KEEPING WATCH

KEEPING WATCH

A WAAF in Bomber Command

Pip Beck

A Goodall paperback
from
Crécy Publishing Limited

First published in Great Britain in 1989 by Goodall Publications Ltd
Reprinted in 2004 by Crécy Publishing Ltd
Reprinted 2012

Front cover photographs from the authors collection

ISBN 9 780907 579380

Printed in Malta by Melita Press

A Goodall paperback
published by
Crécy Publishing Limited
1a Ringway Trading Estate, Shadowmoss Road, Manchester M22 5LH
www.crecy.co.uk

CONTENTS

Poems by Pip Beck

'Darky' Call

Through the static
Loud in my earphones
I heard your cry for aid.
Your scared boy's voice conveyed
Your fear and danger;
Ether-borne, my voice
Went out to you
As lost and in the dark you flew.
We tried so hard to help you,
In your crippled plane -
I called again
But you did not hear.
You had crashed in flame
At the runway's end
With none to tend
You in your dying…

Thoughts on Take-off

They rise, dark-winged,
Mounting the coloured air,
Men and machine to the skies
And the sunset making a glory there.
What are their thoughts,
These men who fly
To the edge of the night
Down the windy sweeps of the sky?
The first faint stars
Are theirs, and below
Lies the darkening land
Where no lights glow.
Our thoughts, like a cloud
Of migrating birds
Fly with them,
Never shaped into words
As they are lost from sight.

A brightness is theirs
Of courage and strength
And each his youth like a brevet wears
Valiant and laughing,
In battle array -
May they safely come back
Before break of day.

More Thoughts

I waved and watched your aircraft thunder past,
Then, circling higher, you were lost,
Anonymous among the multitude of rumbling planes
That streamed across the sunset sky down wide air-lanes.
The momentary gaiety died – I could not call you now.
Abandoned, lonely, how
Should I live the empty hours that loomed before me?
The too-familiar knife lodged in my heart turned cruelly.
I am shut-in – a cold, dark chrysalis encloses me.
When you are back, my dear, I'll be
Alive and warm and gay again,
Forgetting awhile the constant pain of my anxiety.

Preface

This book was written not because I felt that my WAAF experience was more interesting or noteworthy than that of other wartime members of the WAAF. Many have more exciting, or grimmer, or funnier memories than I; I wish they would commit them to paper – I would love to read them.

I wrote it because it was a time in my life when everything was new and exciting; a time I could never forget. A new world opened up, and I would not have missed any of it. Nothing quite like it can happen again because the world has moved on but the good friends I made in those years remain.

Especially I wanted to commemorate those mentioned in the following pages who lost their lives whilst flying. I am proud to have been in their company, and in Bomber Command.

This is one WAAF's story. There may be mistakes and omissions in it, and if so, they are my own. Memory isn't always as reliable as one hopes it is and I hope any errors will be forgiven. Where I've thought embarrassment might be caused to anyone, I have altered names completely.

A short while before his death I was able to give my thanks to Squadron Leader A. G. Goulding DFM for having read my manuscript and having done so felt it was worth recommending to my publisher. And my thanks to Sally MacIntosh, Colin Wallace, DFM, Johnnie Merchant, DFM, Joyce Crooks, Doreen Byrne, and Ivy Draper, and all those who shared their experience with me.

Finally, I wish to reiterate my deep admiration for the men of Bomber Command, who carried the fight to the enemy when no one else could. They were, and are, truly remarkable men.

Pip Beck

I

'Strength Niner, Over'

At last we had arrived. Our van drove over the main road, and RAF Waddington lay before us – an operational bomber station. To the right, over a low hedge, a number of aircraft were parked. I couldn't put a name to them, having only seen one aircraft on the ground in my whole life. It had crash-landed in a field a mile or two from home and my friend Joyce Rogers and I, curious and interested, had cycled out to have a look. We learned from the airman guarding it that it was a Whitley bomber.

Some distance beyond the aircraft immense hangars rose stark against the sky, camouflaged in brown and dull green. Beyond them still, the grassy plain of the airfield stretched away seemingly to the horizon, where the sky was already glowing gold from the lowering sun. On the opposite side of the road we passed numerous houses, each camouflaged like the hangars in sweeps of dull colour. The van stopped outside a larger building, surrounded by tall privet hedges; our driver told us that this was The Waafery. Gathering our belongings together, we thanked him, and as we turned away, a group of sergeants passed us. I knew from the brevets they wore that these were aircrew – the fabulous beings that I admired and hero-worshipped.

For a moment my heart beat a little faster and my imagination took wings – they were young gods and were all about me, though I was earth-bound! Sanity rapidly re-asserted itself, and I blushed for the purple prose of my fancies, heartily thankful that no one could read my thoughts.

We reported to the guard-room at the Waafery and were booked in, thence to the dining-room for a meal. Hungry as wolves, the cheese-on-toast, bread, butter and jam, and copious draughts of tea, were soon disposed of – more than welcome after our early breakfast and the uneatable 'dry (extremely!) rations' with which Bridgnorth had supplied us.

Finally, the Bedding Store issued blankets and sheets, and three weary airwomen were escorted to their quarters in the 'Old

Camp' – two brick huts, side by side. Maureen and I were allotted adjoining beds in one hut. I had taken to Maureen Miller immediately. She was tall, slender and attractive, with thick, honey-coloured hair and green eyes framed with long, black lashes. I guessed her to be a year or two older than myself, with a pleasant manner and an air of gentle, though positive, self-possession. Lorna Cooper was very different – medium height, square-ish build, and dark-mouse hair cut in a square bob, with a sallow complexion, innocent of make-up. She seemed a down-to-earth, no-nonsense kind of person whom I neither liked nor disliked on first acquaintance. Although Joyce and I had joined up at the same time and had gone through initial recruit training at Bridgnorth together, by some administrative slip-up she was posted to a non-operational unit instead of accompanying me to Waddington. Though it was still comparatively early in the evening, we decided to make up our beds and climb in. After our early start, long journey, and the heaving about of heavy kitbags and cases, we were grateful just to lie there and relax between the coarse sheets. We were now quite used to the mattress of three hard 'biscuits', (the Service term for a mattress made up of three separate squares) and the squeaky bolster; I did augment that later with a pillow from home, for extra comfort.

We two didn't have much to say to each other – we were both too sleepy for conversation. I lay lazily trying to take in my new surroundings: the row of black iron bedsteads on either side of the hut, some made up and ready for their owners to slip into, others with 'biscuits' and blankets still stacked in the approved fashion; brown, highly-polished lino covering the floor; dark blue blackout curtains at the windows; photos pinned on the wall over some of the beds as a small personal touch. A few girls were polishing shoes and buttons before going out I supposed. Someone was singing to herself. A small group giggled together round a bed at the end of the hut. Nearer, another girl appeared withdrawn, engrossed in reading a letter of some length.

These details imprinted themselves on my mind with a dreamlike clarity; I was on the verge of sleep. My eyelids drooped. The hut door opened and someone came in. There was a stir of movement about the bed next to mine and I opened my eyes. Glancing at me and seeing that I was awake, the newcomer said, 'hello – you just arrived? I've been here for a fortnight. I'm a parachute-packer – what are you?' Nodding towards Maureen I said, hoping I wouldn't be asked what it entailed, that we were R/T operators. 'Oh?' Her expression was vacant. I was saved explanation by the sudden thunder of aircraft engines overhead. 'Ops tonight,' she said nonchalantly. 'This is a bomber station you know. You'll have a good time here. You can have a different boyfriend every night if you want to – it's wizzo!' 'Wizzo?' I thought, perplexed. I wasn't yet conversant with the details of RAF slang, but I learned rapidly, developing from a snooty *I'm not-going-to-use-those-silly-words* attitude to speaking the 'language' fluently. At intervals the roar of engines continued, as aircraft took-off over the huts. The parachute packer gave herself a quick tidy-up and disappeared, presumably to meet one of the plentiful boyfriends.

I dozed off, thinking about the aircraft that had just left and wondering what part we, as R/T operators, would have in relation to them. For a time, I slept only fitfully, waking with a start when girls came in or went out, but at last the hut was quiet and dark and my sleep sound. Sometime later in the night, I had a vague impression of the noise of engines again mixed up with my dreams.

The next days were occupied with the formalities of 'arriving', during which Maureen, Lorna and I found our way about the camp to the various sections which needed to know of our arrival: the Orderly Room, Pay Accounts, the Gas Section, and numerous others. It was necessary to collect the appropriate number of signatures from the officer or NCO in charge of each section, and a tedious business it was, but at least it enabled us to familiarise ourselves with the camp layout. The aerodrome occupied an area at the base of the triangle of land between the Lincoln-to-Grantham and the Lincoln-to-Sleaford roads. Where we had first entered the camp we now recognised as No 2 barrier and this road was intersected a short distance inside the barrier by a crossroad. Had we continued straight ahead, we would have reached the Sleaford road, passing aircraft dispersals and old hangars and buildings known as 'FMU', which I guessed to be 'Field Maintenance Unit'.

The main road through the camp was the left-hand turn of the crossroad, and it divided the domestic side of the station from the airfield and operational side, curving away past the Officers' Mess and the Transmitting Station and out to the Lincoln-Grantham road again at the northern boundary. This was No 1 barrier. Returning to the crossroads, the grassy lane on the corner of which the Old Camp stood led away to the south. This was part of Ermine Street – the old Roman road which cut its way through the counties – sometimes, as here, a grassy forgotten way, sometimes almost obliterated, sometimes incorporated into a modern road. But our length of the road was Green Lane, and there was no barrier across it. Some distance along, it joined a metalled road, but until then, was quiet between low hedges and occasional taller trees, a haven for walking or cycling. It had an indefinable atmosphere of otherness, and I loved it. It was to become a favourite haunt and I never tired of wandering along the peaceful stretch of it, sometimes with friends I was yet to meet, sometimes alone. Cecil, Sally and Joan, Frank, James. Green Lane would hold many memories for me, wrapped in its leafy silences. Just as it had held a myriad of other memories for more than a thousand years.

The arrival formalities finally completed, we reported back to the WAAF guardroom, wondering what came next. We supposed we would be introduced to our place of work. Our documents described us as 'RTOs', and because of this, we were almost packed off to the Orderly Room to learn to peruse train time-tables and absorb other information necessary for the training of Railway Transport Officers! We managed to disabuse the WAAF Admin staff of this idea, and having a vague notion that SHQ Signals might be a possibility, suggested that we try there since the Waafery clearly had no clue as to what to do with us. We were unique of our kind on the station though not for long as it turned out; we were also, we later learned, among the first of the WAAF R/T operators in 5 Group.

Hopefully, we went over to SHQ, and waited in the olive-green corridor outside the Signals Officer's office – only to find that we were not needed there either. We began to feel unwanted.

Finally the Signals Officer established for us that we were to work in what he called the Watch Office. This he pointed out – a square, box-like building standing in front of the hangars on the airfield perimeter – and yet again we set off. We entered a door behind the sandbagged blast-wall, and ascended concrete steps that led to a partially glass-panelled door; here we paused, our hearts beating a little faster with nervous anticipation; then one of us knocked resolutely, and we walked in.

Seated at a table to our right, was an officer wearing the rings of a squadron leader. We approached him, saluted, and explained who we were. Once more we were met with a nonplussed manner – no one had told him of our arrival, and he hum-ed and ha-ed a little about what to do with us? Then he made the best suggestion we had heard so far. 'Would you like a weekend's leave?' he enquired. 'That will give us the chance to sort you out.' Leave, so soon! 'Oh yes – thank you, sir,' we chorused – and back we pelted to the WAAF guardroom to find out what was required in order to go home. We received some sour looks from one or two of the admin staff, but were told to go to the Orderly Room, where we were duly initiated into the ritual for obtaining the magic form 295. Light-hearted and happy as I was, it didn't worry me too much that I hadn't enough money for my fare. We had so far had only one pay-day, and 14 shillings a fortnight didn't go far (I had made an allotment of half my pay to my mother). I decided to hitchhike. Remembering a large map of England on a wall in SHQ Signals, I went over to study it. Lofty, a friendly corporal, helped me to plan a route on hearing of my intention. Next morning we were off: Maureen and Lorna going to Lincoln and I in the opposite direction, to Grantham. Where was all the traffic, I wondered?

I caught a bus; this wasn't how it was supposed to be. In Grantham, I paused for a cup of tea in a café, and at a nearby table noticed an RAF corporal, poring over a map. I'd already seen a little red two-seater parked outside, and decided it must belong to him. But dare I ask him, and enquire in what direction he was heading? Well, I'd better make up my mind quickly as he was already folding his map and calling for his bill. He looked pleasant – I would chance it. Strange to think that a few short weeks ago, I wouldn't have dreamed of doing such a thing; being in the Services changed all that.

I made my enquiry: he smiled, not minding, and told me he could take me as far as Huntingdon, if I was ready to leave. I was and we were soon speeding through the late summer countryside, the wind blowing through my hair. I kept my cap on my knee. I would probably have lost it to the breeze otherwise. It was a wonderfully exhilarating drive, and the first time I had ever ridden in a sports car; I was sorry to leave it when we arrived at Huntingdon, but a good part of my journey was accomplished. I was rather self-conscious about thumbing a lift, and compromised by putting up a tentative hand when a car or lorry approached on the outskirts of the town. I soon got a lift, and then another, and a third – all of which took me to St Neots, then Bedford – where I saw a bus going to Buckingham; I had just enough money for the fare. When I walked in, my parents' astonished expressions were a joy to behold. They had not expected to see me again for weeks, or more likely, months. Yet to me, that August morning when Joyce and I had departed seemed ages ago. So much had happened: so much to tell, and the next day, I went to see Joyce's parents, and told it all over again. Then, I was on my way back, returning to Lincoln more decorously by train, at my mother's insistence. I now knew I could get a bus from Lincoln to Waddington – no one in their right mind went to Waddington by rail. Arrangements had been made for us to start work at last, and I was looking forward zestfully to learning the rudiments of my new job. We were told that five RAF R/T operators worked at the Watch Office, though one was at present on leave. Each operator, covering the 24 hours worked a shift system consisting of a four-hour watch and an eight-hour watch. If we were lucky enough to have a full complement of operators, we all had a day off between each twelve-hour day. If not, we had every third day off, after an eight-hour night duty. This, of course, continued day in and day out, except for leave.

I liked the thought of watch-keeping, and time off during the day – though I wondered if I'd be able to keep awake all night. The three of us were taken up to the Watch Office roof to see where we would be working. The R/T cabin seemed incredibly tiny; half its space was taken up by a broad bench along the back wall which housed two identical radio sets – 'TR9s', we were told – though this conveyed precisely nothing to us just then. There was a microphone like an upright telephone, and the airman on duty was wearing earphones from which, as we listened fascinated, came the sound of a blurred voice. I couldn't make out the message, but the operator grasped the microphone and, moving a lever on the TR9, said, 'Hello Lighthouse L-London, this is Jetty answering, receiving you loud and clear, strength niner, over.' As he spoke, he wrote rapidly in a logbook on the bench. I wondered what 'strength niner' was. And then I thought – so this is what our 'clear voices' was all about – we would be speaking to aircraft with the aid of a microphone, perhaps, when they came back from a raid? If so – this was everything I'd hoped for, and more. I couldn't wait to get started.

My first watch the next morning was from 08.00 hrs until 13.00 and then 16.30 to 23.59 – midnight. Joe Rodgers was my tutor and watch-companion – a pleasant, calm Yorkshireman in his early thirties – which, to me at 18, seemed positively middle-aged. The impression was heightened by his curly brown hair which was beginning to grey and recede at the temples. But Joe was good-natured and patient, with a quiet sense of humour, instructing me carefully in this element so completely new and strange.

I learned about procedure: the set replies and instructions to use in any contingency by both air and ground operators; the phonetic alphabet: A-Apple, B-Beer, C-Charles, and so on. This was updated from time to time. And signal strengths, which could be anything from 'strength 2' – very faint – to 'strength niner', which was the loudest signal. 'Niner' was 9, and so pronounced as to distinguish it from '5' – 'fife' – as the two words could easily be confused on R/T.

The mysteries began to unravel. All R/T conversations had to be logged and the necessary abbreviations memorised. The act of transmitting consisted only of pushing a small lever from the 'receive' position to 'transmit', but Joe told me we would later be taught the technicalities of our job and there would be much to learn. We would also be required to signal morse code by Aldis lamp. It all sounded rather formidable, but I was certain I'd be able to cope with it – given time. I already knew Morse code, more or less – Joyce and I had asked a neighbour, who happened to be the commandant of Buckingham's Home Guard, to give us lessons whilst we waited to be called-up, and he had obliged.

As the first weeks passed, I began to be familiar with the station routine. I rapidly learned that it was a good thing to keep out of the way of the WAAF Admin staff, from our CO down. I had already been admonished by the WAAF CO for attempting to enter the Waafery by the front door, in ignorance that its use was reserved for officers and senior NCOs. My place had been made very clear: the *back* entry was for WAAFs like me – *never* the front. As I had only so recently arrived, it would be overlooked this time. Otherwise I would have been put on a charge. It wasn't a very good start. The Watch Office became my world, and I loved being on duty there. I learned what an ops – operations – night was like, with all the tension and anxiety it generated, and the relief if all the aircraft returned safely; or the sad, empty feeling if someone was missing. So far the crews were just names on a battle-order to me – we saw little of them from our roof-top eyrie, so I did not yet experience a personal grief for those who failed to return.

I had one encounter with a pilot I had met at a dance at home, before I became a WAAF. He had danced with me a lot, but when I mentioned that I was waiting to join the WAAF, he had been disapproving. Suddenly turning a corner and coming face to face with him here at Waddington, I had cried 'Gerry!' with surprise and pleasure, but he had turned a cold face towards me, and though he politely asked me how I was, went on to announce that his opinion of the WAAF had not changed, and it now applied to me also. He walked off leaving me standing in confusion and embarrassment. The incident had hurt. 'So much for my "Young gods",' I thought ruefully.

Still – surely they couldn't all think alike? At least the men who were R/T operators did not. Admittedly a female intrusion into the Watch Office had not been greeted initially with any enthusiasm, though there were WAAFs in the Met Office below, but they kept themselves decently out of the way. However, we seemed to have made a place for ourselves. It was agreed that we applied ourselves to our job, and were not really too bad; it was even admitted that we brightened the place up – and of course, we made tea. Genuinely friendly relationships developed between all of us: Joe, with whom I still shared a watch; Mac, a tall Scot with a lined, rather anxious face, from Edinburgh; Jock, nineteen years old, from a Scottish border-town; and Jack, an ex-schoolteacher and rampant Socialist. Or perhaps he was a Communist – I knew very little of politics, but Jack spoke his mind on the subject with some fervour. Finally, there was Ken, a good-looking fair-haired boy who lived-out at his home in Lincoln. Also there were the wireless operators who manned the Guard and Safety wave W/T sets in a room behind the Control Office, when ops were on. The men R/T operators were on friendly terms with them – particularly Vin, who went around with Joe and Jock. It wasn't long before Maureen and I were included in their outings to Lincoln for a meal or to see a film; we were introduced to Mrs Holden's café near the Stonebow, where we consumed many an enjoyable meal of fish and Mrs H's special, crinkle-cut chips. I was always hungry. Perhaps it was because of the meals we missed whilst sleeping after night duty. I found a little café on Silver Street which sold waffles with maple syrup; deliciously sweet and available any time – my private treat. Vin invited me to go swimming one mild evening. I hadn't brought a swimsuit with me, but was offered the loan of one by Sheila, one of my roommates (as shift-workers, we had recently been moved into pre-war married quarters – much to be preferred to the huts of the Old Camp). Sheila produced the swimsuit from my inspection. 'Gosh! Are you sure you don't mind my borrowing it?' I asked. I wouldn't have wanted to lend it to anyone. It was beautiful: perfectly cut and pale orange-gold with a subtle sheen. In short, a very expensive costume. 'No – I have several – don't worry about it,' she said.

Sheila was slim, dark and sophisticated, with a cynical air. She was already in her 20s and came from a well-connected Irish family, though no trace of accent intruded in her speech. She possessed her own privately tailored uniform; it had never occurred to me that anyone might actually *buy* their own uniform! Beside her bed, in a silver frame, was a photo of her Army officer fiancé – a romance which had its ups and downs, if her occasional references to him were anything to go by. 'Really! He's so stupidly unreasonable – he doesn't seem to realise that I'm in the Services too!' I didn't know what it was all about. I was delighted with her generous loan of the swimsuit though. Vin seemed impressed by it too. He was a farmer in civilian life – a shy man, with a sort of sweet simplicity and a niceness which appealed to me. He soon departed from the Watch Office orbit though. A few weeks later he was posted to the Middle East.

I experienced my first air-raid whilst on duty one evening in September. We were in the middle of landing ops when we received the air raid warning Red, and bombs began dropping almost immediately. The airfield lights were doused, and our own aircraft had to circle in darkness after being warned of an intruder in the circuit – which must have been fairly obvious. We realised it was just one enemy aircraft dropping a stick of bombs across the airfield, but the explosions were getting nearer. An almighty 'Crump!' was very close, and the Watch Office shook. I wasn't the only one to believe the next bomb would be for us. The Senior Control Officer, who was in the cabin with us, flattened himself against the wall. My mind seemed suddenly quite blank, as I logged the anxious questions from our aircraft, and Joe's answers. The thought briefly flitted across my consciousness that it was a pity I was going to die so soon – my parents would be very upset; it was a mere flicker over the void. But the next bomb didn't come; the raider had departed. Immediately the airfield sprang to life – runway lights were re-lit, and the Control Officer did a hasty inspection of the runway areas for damage, but reported them fit for use. There was a large crater between the Watch Office and No. 3 hangar though.

Landings were restarted, and continued as rapidly as possible. Some of our aircraft were desperately short of fuel. Finally, all were down safely, on almost empty tanks.

Joe and I could at last sit back and relax, and Joe turned to me, saying, 'You know, Phyl, I was proud of you – you were so calm you gave *me* courage!' But I had been merely petrified, and the thought of *that* giving Joe courage made me laugh. Laughing gave way to violent shivering – I couldn't stop my teeth chattering – and I was grateful for the cup of hot tea Joe then made for me, which helped to reduce my nervous reaction. Still – it *was* rather exciting. Several people had told me about a raid earlier in 1941, when there had been a direct hit on a slit trench where some NAAFI girls, the NAAFI manageress, and a sergeant-pilot had been sheltering. All were killed. People were still shocked by this tragedy. The village church in Waddington was destroyed by a landmine about the same time. Well, if there had to be bombs, I knew where I'd prefer to be – on duty at the Watch Office. I didn't fancy trenches and shelters.

The Waafery notice board announced that a dance was to be held in the Sergeants' Mess. I consulted Maureen, as we were both off duty that evening, and we decided to go. We took considerable trouble getting ready, in happy anticipation. 'Best blues' were pressed, and buttons polished until they shone like silver – we'd already discovered that using Silvo rather than Brasso helped in this illusion. Shoes gleamed; our shirts and collars freshly laundered; and stockings clean, but indisputably lisle. We had not yet realised that at our own expense, we could buy silk (but strictly forbidden) stockings, and also the far smarter Van Heusen collars – if fortunate enough to be able to scrounge some clothing coupons. This problem was solved when a small issue of coupons was made to the WAAF, officially to buy handkerchiefs and other non-issue items. I don't think silk stockings had been envisaged as among these by the authorities, but they certainly were by us. Maureen and I had both washed and set our hair, combing it down just a little longer than was permissible, so that it curled on our collar and below our ears. I enjoyed the sensation of shaking my head and feeling my hair swing softly, loose from the dark ribbon I usually wore, tucking my hair round it and making a roll along sides and back.

Finally, there was make-up. Maureen had introduced me to the practice of buying theatrical greasepaint for lipstick and eye shadow, as it was much cheaper than commercial make-up, and used with care, looked very natural. I remembered a remark of Jock's, a few days earlier. He had looked at me critically and then said, 'You know – if only you'd a wee bit more colour, you'd be quite pretty!' So I'd *have* a bit more colour, I blended a spot of greasepaint along my cheekbone very carefully, and surveyed the effect. Yes – I thought it was better; and Maureen agreed. Then the last touch – a dab of perfume – the ubiquitous 'Evening in Paris'. Half the WAAF section must have wafted into the dance wearing it. Spare cash didn't run to anything more expensive and desirable. We were ready.

At the Sergeants' Mess we made our way to where the action seemed to be. This was in a large hall; the dining room I imagined, cleared of its chairs and tables and now crowded with dancing couples. The air was already thick with cigarette smoke and a strong smell of beer pervaded the atmosphere near the bar. The whole place throbbed with talk and laughter and the beat of the band. Maureen was invited to dance almost immediately, and disappeared into the throng. I, knowing no one and feeling shy, self-conscious and conspicuous standing alone, lost my nerve, and fled before the dance ended, searching for cover. I found it behind a door marked 'Ante-room', which I cautiously opened. It seemed to be a lounge, with armchairs and small tables round the sides of the room. A few sergeants sitting about reading magazines or papers, glanced up as I entered, but no one said anything, so I assumed it was alright for me to be there. It didn't occur to me that they might have retired there to escape the WAAF invasion! I sank into an armchair and picked up a magazine – was it 'Tee Emm'? I wasn't at all sure what I was looking at; I almost decided to leave and go back to the billet. If only I knew someone, just to exchange a few words with. Suddenly, a voice said, 'Come on, woman, smile – this is supposed to be a party!'

A tall sergeant was standing in front of my chair, and it was he who had spoken. He beckoned a passing waiter, and asked what I'd like to drink. 'Sherry,' I said hesitantly, unable to think of anything else, and the waiter brought it. My new acquaintance seated himself in the next chair, and I saw that he wore an airgunner's brevet and wireless operator's badge. 'You're new here, aren't you?' he enquired. 'I don't think I've seen you around before. Look – I'm a bit tight just now, but I promise I won't drink any more if you'll come and dance with me!' I finished my sherry and followed him to the dance-floor, where we danced close in the crush of couples, the smoky air making my eyes tingle.

The smell of alcohol near the bar was now overpowering, and the floor wet with spilt beer. We kept away from that area as much as possible, and my partner stuck to his promise and drank no more. He told me that his name was Ron Atkinson, and his home was in Hull. We danced and danced – I was having a wonderful time. Sometimes, we slipped back to the ante-room again, just to talk. He teased me, and we both laughed a lot. I studied his angular, intelligent face and large grey eyes; the dark hair and rather youthful moustache – perhaps the most youthful thing about him. At twenty-one – he told me his age – no hint of callowness remained; this much I sensed without, yet, fully appreciating the reasons. We fell in love – what else would we do? But it was an anxiety-ridden time. When he was flying and I was on duty, I would listen on R/T for the accents of Pete, his Rhodesian pilot, as the time for their return approached, willing them back. When at last Pete's voice came over the air, the swelling balloon of anxiety in my mind would collapse and shrivel away to nothing, and be forgotten – until next time. Which wasn't long in coming. We were not often free at the same time, and chafed at our inability to meet as often as we'd like. Then Ron asked me to marry him. Marriage was something I hadn't thought about. I was just in love. Romance was all I had needed; marriage was serious, and I didn't feel *old* enough. I tried to explain how I felt to Ron. But to him, it appeared that I was rebuffing him – and he turned away, hurt and angry.

We didn't see each other for three days, and I was miserable and unhappy. Then I ran into him as I left the cookhouse after tea. He was wearing battle-dress, flying boots, thick white roll-necked pullover – and a little black cat charm dangling from the button of his breast pocket. So he was 'on' tonight. My anxieties rose in full force – and yet I felt a surge of fierce pride. I suppose women down the ages have felt the same urgent emotions, as they watched their fighting men go off to war. 'Phyl – I'm so glad I've seen you. I was going to leave a message for you in Control. Phone me tomorrow afternoon in the Mess – I must talk to you – it's important. I have to go now – I'm on my way to briefing. Listen out for me tonight, won't you?' Of course I would. I'd be on duty all night. But I felt a chill – and there'd been no time even to touch hands. I couldn't shake off a sense of foreboding, even though I reminded myself it was always like this.

Ron's crew had had to make a last-minute change of aircraft, from W-William to H-Harry; I knew they wouldn't be happy about that – they always flew in W-William and trusted it. They hated flying in anything else. It wasn't a good start to this trip to Le Havre, the target. The night seemed endless as the dark hours dragged past, slowly, slowly. Sometimes I lifted the blanket which blacked out our door, and walked out on to the roof, staring into the cloudy night and trying to reassure myself that Ron's aircraft was still flying somewhere in that vast sky; of course it was. The squadron was due to return about 06.00 hrs. The Control tower roof filled up with those concerned for the fate of our aircraft, and we all waited for the first contact. It came, followed by others. No H-Harry yet. I began to get a cold, shrinking feeling in the pit of my stomach, and had to fight down my anxiety and panic – force myself to concentrate on logging accurately. Then all were back except H-Harry. Maybe they had landed elsewhere? That must be it. The squadron commander voiced this possibility to the Control officer, which temporarily heartened me. But there had been no phone call by 08.00 hrs when I was due to go off duty, and now I knew there wouldn't be.

Fresh operators came on duty, and I hung behind, standing again on the roof alone, trying to pierce the opaque whiteness of the morning sky. Tears spilled from my eyes and I left quickly, running back to the billet and privacy. I telephoned the Sergeants' Mess that afternoon – just in case – but an impersonal voice told me that Sergeant Atkinson wasn't there –

no, they hadn't seen him – and my last hope was gone. Loss was an unknown experience until now – and it was painful. I didn't talk about it to anyone, and tried to behave normally. I was silently grateful to those who *did* know, and were unobtrusively kind. And at eighteen, one recovers quickly.

2

Airborne!

Changes took place in the Watch Office. When I had first worked there, it was Regional Control. Now, it was to be known as Flying Control and a new squadron leader came to take over. There had been a great flood of u/t, under-training, R/T operators in the past few weeks, and conditions in our roof-top cabin had been congested if not claustrophobic, with up to five people squashed into it on most watches; rather like an over-crowded lift.

Our new Senior Flying Control Officer pulled strings, and the influx ceased. Surplus numbers were gradually posted to other stations. Alas – Maureen and Lorna were among the postings, and I missed them, being now the sole surviving member of the original three. The three girls remaining were Pat, Vera, and Jane. Pat and Vera became great friends. Both must have been the joy of any WAAF officer looking for a perfectly turned-out WAAF. Tidy, well-pressed, buttons gleaming, hair neat – Pat's hair was red-gold, Vera's dark blonde, and if anyone had an 'English rose' complexion, Vera surely did. Pat – from Newcastle – was very quiet. Her fiancé was a POW, and the thought of the unguessably-long separation must have oppressed her deeply. Jane was a different type entirely: short bleached-blonde hair and eyebrows plucked to a thin line and pencilled black; deep blue eyes with black mascared lashes; eyes, as rapidly became evident, wise in the ways of men.

The rest of us, less sophisticated, watched with interest. Another of our new squadron leader's moves had been to bring us and our R/T sets down to the main Flying Control office – a move not at first viewed with favour by us as we felt we had lost a small freedom – we would now be continually under supervision. We quickly got used to it, however, and had to admit that it was a much more efficient arrangement. Jane made the best of it. She would bring her embroidery with her on a quiet evening or night watch, spreading her hanks of coloured silk about the desk – and wait. Sooner or later, an aircrew officer would appear, and Jane would add a stitch or two to her pattern and flash her blue eyes in his direction. After a brief word with the FCO – his excuse for the visit – he would slip into a chair beside her and chat for a while, then leave. This was followed by a discreet exit on Jane's part – and no Jane for a while, a situation that wasn't allowed to continue. I heard F/Lt Hobson say, in great indignation, 'What does she think this is – a bloody knocking-shop!' I hadn't heard the expression before, but was wary of asking what it meant. I had the glimmering of an idea.

The Station Commander came up to Control one evening when Jane's silks were spread around. He ordered them to be removed at once, and forbade anything of this nature to be brought on duty by R/T operators in future. A few endless hours with nothing to do but make tea, between ops leaving and returning, drove us to finding ways around his edict. We stuffed our respirator cases (minus gasmasks) with letters to write or books to read or study – things that could be quickly hidden away under the logbook or pushed back into the case. Then Jane was posted – and Jane legends abounded for a while. Knitting unobtrusively reappeared, as well as letters and books. Even sewing – though this was often done for one or other of the Control Officers, when they found we didn't mind – or most of us didn't – and were quite capable. At various times, I sewed on buttons; changed sleeve-braid after a promotion; turned shirt-cuffs; even darned socks in an emergency. For these small services we were always thanked gratefully.

The interior of Flying Control was again re-planned. Now, the R/T operators and TR9s were positioned at the bench which ran across the centre of the office, directly overlooking the airfield. The corner we had briefly occupied before now had a door knocked through the wall to the room behind. This had earlier housed the Guard and Safety Wave W/T sets and their operators. On busy nights whilst waiting for ops to return, it had not been unusual for one of the R/T operators to snatch an hour or so's 'kip' on a set of biscuits behind the tall power-packs near the wall that was now partly demolished. The chattering Morse keys had formed a background to our doze. Now the sets, no longer used, had vanished and the operators, including dear, shy Vin, posted overseas. There was an exception though. This was Pat, a big man with dark wavy hair and light green eyes, who had been an actor at the Old Vic. He had gone on an AG's course and would go on to become aircrew; I hoped he would be able to return to the Old Vic some day. There were to be maps, charts and reference books in the new office, and wooden models of aircraft – our own, and German types – suspended from the ceiling for recognition practice. I became fascinated by these, and observed them from all angles; I rather fancied myself on aircraft recognition.

Our new situation at the Control bench was next to the wind-indicator at the end, to our left. The TR9s were installed under the bench and operated by remote push-button control. This was a considerable improvement on the transmit/receive lever we had hitherto used, and which frequently gave us mild electric shocks no matter how many times the radio mechanics were called to service them. A loudspeaker was incorporated and crackled and muttered away in front of us, but was invaluable when operations were returning. At the far end of the bench, next to the airfield lighting layout panel, which could be illuminated, stood another loudspeaker. This was tuned to Coastal Command's 'Darky' frequency, but we never had a call on it. Police car transmissions occasionally echoed disconcertingly from it, but Coastal Command ignored us and after a time the speaker disappeared.

An item which did not disappear but became a standard Flying Control fitting throughout Bomber Command, with minor variations, was Flight Lieutenant Button's board. F/Lt Button was, like Hobby, an RFC veteran pilot. The board was divided into sections and showed the position of each aircraft on the circuit, and the height it had been given; whether the aircraft was airborne but out of the area, ie, operating or on a cross-country flight, or if it was on the ground. The squadrons were differentiated by buttons of contrasted colours, each with an aircraft letter, so that when ops were landing, a glance at the button-board showed exactly what the situation was. Originally we had jotted all this down on scraps of paper, and been subject to spells of blind panic if anyone inadvertently moved or covered up our precious list! We didn't know if the button-board was named after its originator, or simply because it was a board for buttons – but we felt F/Lt Button should have the honour. The board was built into the desk next to our loudspeaker. Next to this was one of the gadgets which was the pride and joy of our new squadron leader – a ten-line tieline telephone link with Group, the Station Commander, DF, Station Sick-quarters, among others. We soon learned to operate this; it was simple and very useful.

The second gadget which so delighted our SFCO was a loaded spring-arm for automatically shutting the Control office door. Visitors had a distressing habit of leaving it open behind them, to the discomfort of the occupants, especially in cold weather. It was fitted with due ceremony, and it so happened that the first person to come in afterwards was the Group Captain. 'Come in' is perhaps not a good description. He was catapulted in. The spring appeared to be working in reverse, and at his firm pressure on the handle the door burst open – and stayed open – and the GC ended up almost lying across the bench, propelled by his forward momentum.

There was a stunned silence for a few seconds, during which I doubt if I was the only one trying to suppress hysterical giggles. Utter consternation showed on the rotund and normally cheerful features of our squadron leader; no doubt the thought of several ghastly fates was going through his mind – a posting to the Shetland Isles, perhaps? The Group Captain rose to his full height with what dignity he could muster – and he was a dignified man. He delivered a short but pithy comment regarding the correct fitting of the spring-arm and departed. Someone from Works and Bricks was hastily summoned, and the job done properly in double-quick time. We all watched the door apprehensively for the remainder of the afternoon.

Our technical training was progressing and we – the u/t operators – would go to the transmitting station several times a week for instruction. At first our eyes were drawn to the tall transmitters humming ceaselessly in the otherwise quiet room, their large valves glowing blue. Occasional flickering and clicking showed them to be in use, as we discovered later. The floor was highly polished and there were duckboards between the rows of transmitters. The atmosphere was pleasantly warm; a soothing place for learning.

Dave, the little Scots corporal, and LAC 'Smudge' Smith were our teachers. They were very patient with us. They needed to be. We were required to know about electronic theory and Ohms Law; primary and secondary cells; the charging of accumulators and their care; the Type 'B' charging board (I wondered if there were any other types – we were never told); magnetism; valve theory; simple circuits, including capacity, inductance, resistance and couplings; wave-forms; and aerials and their care. We had already been instructed pretty thoroughly in the manipulation of the TR9 by Joe and the other R/T ops, as well as in faults, minor repairs and DIs. We were shown how to DI aircraft R/T too, though in practice we never did so. We also learned how to solder, which I liked, enjoying the aroma of the flux and the delicate manipulation of the iron. All very basic stuff to the average wireless op or mechanic, but strange and esoteric to us. The mysteries were slowly unravelled for us by Dave and Smudge. We compiled 'gen' books and consulted these at every opportunity. We were all keen to do well at the Board whenever the examiners should come our way – a matter very much in the lap of the gods it seemed.

I loved the open view across the airfield which we now enjoyed from Control during the day. The outlook took on an immense attraction for me and I never tired of the great flat space of green which stretched to the horizon, broken only by a few distant trees and some old buildings: the limitless arc of the sky. I saw it at all times of the day and night now. As the pale primrose of dawn spread up the early grey, in the short space of quiet between the welcome return of our aircraft and the beginning of a new day; and when the west flamed with sunset colours. I saw it silent and silver under a full moon, and noisy and flashing with activity on a busy night; lowering and grey under threatening cloud-cover, with rain squalls sweeping across the deserted expanse and expending their force in streams down the Watch Office windows. I saw it shrouded in fog and eerily still – a strange no-place – and later, in winter, smooth and white and brilliant with snow. At least, until the snow ploughs and diggers of all ranks got to work to clear a runway.

Usually, there was the normal mixture of cloud, sun, wind and rain, and aircraft taking-off or landing. 44 Squadron's Hampdens and 207 Squadron's Manchesters, air testing or operating, 1506 Blind Approach Training Flight's Oxfords, flying daily. Aircraft from other stations dropped in too, Tiger Moths, Whitleys, Wellingtons – once a Stirling landed, huge and gawky on the ground. 207 Squadron departed for Bottesford in mid November, leaving behind the legend of Flight Lieutenant 'Kipper' Herring – the first pilot ever to bring home a Manchester on one engine. For this astonishing feat, he was awarded the DSO. Even I, who knew little enough about the aircraft I saw, had heard about the Manchester's dicey reputation.

Jock and I were sharing an afternoon duty when a message was delivered to Flying Control which gave us cause for great rejoicing. It originated from BAT Flight and said that any R/T operators who wished to gain experience of their job from the air were welcome to fly as passengers with BAT Flight details. Jock and I exchanged jubilant glances; we both knew where we were going the moment we went off duty. Tea could wait. We dashed round to No. 1 hangar and presented ourselves at the Flight Office, panting. The New Zealand squadron leader – his red hair matched by a bristling moustache – received us with some surprise and amusement. He admitted he had not expected such an immediate response, and seemed even more surprised to see me – a WAAF. We were in luck. Two aircraft were due to take off in the next few minutes. We went to the crew-room to draw parachutes – though there was no time for instruction in their use – and to sign the 'Blood Book', which I understood was to absolve the RAF from blame should the aircraft crash and kill us! Jock's aircraft was pointed out to him, at the far end of the concrete apron outside the hangar, and the squadron leader motioned me to follow him to the aircraft he was about to take up. I was light-headed with excitement and nervous tension and the parachute felt funny, bumping the backs of my legs as I walked. The Flight Commander and his pupil climbed up into the Oxford, and I followed, awkward in my skirt, and settled myself on the step behind the cockpit. He turned to me with a grin: 'If you feel sick whilst we're up, just point down and I'll land!'

He started the engines and we taxied round the perimeter track to the beginning of the runway, paused for cockpit checks, and then we were away, speeding down the runway. I became suddenly aware that we were no longer in contact with the ground, and rising higher each moment. Now we could see the whole aerodrome beneath us. For the first time in my life I was airborne! We circled, gaining height, and the hangars and buildings became tiny models, the roofs of Waddington village, warm spots of colour in the patchwork of varied browns and greens which were the surrounding fields. Roads were grey ribbons dividing and binding the spreading landscape below. I was entranced, with never a thought of my usual horror of heights. We entered a thick layer of cloud – a strange experience to be surrounded by opaque whiteness, with no sense of direction or movement. At least the pupil-pilot who had now taken over the controls knew, since that was the purpose of the exercise, to stay on course in conditions of poorest visibility.

The vapour thinned – and we were in bright sunlight and blue skies. Higher and higher we rose, and the giant cumulus tops rose with us like cotton-wool mountain peaks, above the rippled layer of stratus below and dazzling white. It was an enchanted world, in which other aircraft came and went along the sky-lanes, and I recognised some of our own Hampdens and Manchesters airtesting. I gave little thought, though, to anything else except the magical impressions flowing into my consciousness. I had no idea how long we'd been airborne, but when we began to descend into cloud again I glanced at my watch and realised that almost an hour had passed. We came out below the cloud-layer and there was the airfield below, so we'd be landing presently, I thought regretfully.

But I had one more experience still to come. The squadron leader turned and motioned me to exchange places with the pupil-pilot, who also handed me his helmet. I moved into his seat at the dual controls and plugged in the helmet.

'Now – *you* are going to fly the aircraft!' I was told. If my heart rate could have been monitored in the next few minutes, it would probably have gone off the clock. 'You can take over the controls now – I'll tell you what to do,' said my pilot. 'Push the stick forward – gently – gently – now level out.' He showed me how to keep the aircraft straight and level with the aid of the artificial horizon, and it looked so easy until I tried it; the 'wings' on the instrument bounced up and down in spite of all my efforts to keep them steady. I was next instructed to push the rudder-bar with my foot, and found the Oxford banking towards the airfield; so fascinated was I by this manoeuvre that I almost forgot to ease my foot off. 'Straighten her up, like you did before,' I was told. My earthward-pointing wing tip gradually levelled up again. 'Call up Control and ask permission to land!' Well, I knew how to do that at least. I did so, and it was odd hearing Pat's voice on the R/T giving permission to pancake. 'Right – good! You've brought her to the runway approach – now I'll take over.' And we were gliding down toward the runway. I sat back for a few moments. I *had* flown an Oxford – well, only for a few minutes – but still, I had flown it! My skin felt stretched and thin with excitement.

There was a gentle bump as we touched down, and the runway flowed beneath our wheels once more. We taxied up to the hangar. 'Come into the office and have a cup of tea,' the squadron leader said. I think he had enjoyed the novelty almost as much as I and I beamed joyously. Jock followed a few moments later, and we gratefully downed cups of tea, recollecting that we'd had none. We thanked the New Zealander enthusiastically, and he said we were welcome to go again, anytime. We left, feeling euphoric. I could have danced all the way to the cookhouse, where we consumed a cold and congealing meal, barely noticing what we ate.

I tried later, when alone, to collect my impressions of this first flight. How was it that I, normally terrified of heights, could look down to earth, perhaps three thousand feet below and be unafraid? What I *had* felt was the extraordinary sensation of being free of earth – of exploring this new dimension, the sky, and the immense freedom of space, sunlight, cloud; all this in just an hour – sixty minutes of wonder.

3

The Rhodesians

44 Squadron had become 44 (Rhodesia) Squadron in September 1941, because of the considerable number of Rhodesian volunteers now serving with it, many awaiting aircrew training. Of their number was Cecil – named like quite a lot of his compatriots, after the founder of their country. (Why did it have to be Cecil? Why not John or Richard or Christopher Rhodes? Well, too late to complain now, I supposed.)

Cecil had known Ron because of Ron's Rhodesian pilot, Peter Bell, and soon after Ron went missing, he had seen me in the bus-station at Lincoln and had come over gently to express his sympathy. Since then we had met around the camp though mostly in the NAAFI or the cookhouse, where for some weeks the WAAF and airmen had dined together, at first partially segregated, but that ruling had been rescinded. The increasing numbers of WAAF arriving at the station had crowded out our original small dining-room at the Waafery. So, if Cecil met me outside the cookhouse, I'd find myself seated at a table full of Rhodesians, or I'd be invited to join the after-lunch throng in the hall between the mess and the NAAFI to drink tea.

The Rhodesians were so unmistakably not English; their appearance was often highly individual during working time at least, with sheepskin jerkins worn over tunics and roll-neck pullovers; cap-comforters in place of forage caps, and battered flying boots or rolled-down wellington boots with thick white socks inside. Of course, our own ground-crew resorted to similar clothing out on the flights, but the Rhodesians managed to make it look far more outlandish, with their air of tough independence, skins bronzed by warmer sun than ours, and eyes used to wider distances. Their independence and disregard for the finer points of discipline was a by-word on the camp.

Their accent was clipped and unfamiliar, and their speech sprinkled with words or phrases in Afrikaans. 'Tot siens' they would say when they were leaving friends, as we would say

'Cheerio.' And to Sandy, a mongrel adopted by the groundcrews, 'Vutsak!' if he ran after them at inappropriate moments. I assumed it meant 'go away'. Crew transports were 'gharries' – everyone else used the term too.

I liked their easy, pleasant manner and lack of formality, and soon came to know them well, introduced by Cecil. I met Alec, a tall blond, handsome boy and 'Shadow', even taller, and though broad-shouldered, very slimly built, hence the nickname. Then Van, Bob, Mac, Pat, Tommy, Army and more Cecils. Men who came from places with strange musical names: Shangani, Umtali, Gwelo, Selukwe, Que-Que, Bulawayo – one could almost make a song from them I thought. Salisbury was less unfamiliar. Being ever-intrigued with faraway places, I was a good listener when they talked of home, and became fascinated by what I learned of their country. They had one deep resentment against this country – it was that they were still a colony and not a dominion. This rankled greatly (ironic shades of things to come). To stress their protest at this state of affairs, they filed off the crown above the Rhodesian lion on their cap-badge. It was one way of registering independence! Yet they still chose to come over to England to fight and fly.

Over a lunch-time cup of tea Cecil told me he had volunteered for pilot-training and passed the medical and other preliminary tests in Rhodesia, but as there were no immediate vacancies on the course, he had asked to come to this country as a fitter whilst he waited. In civilian life, he was a mining engineer. His home was in Que-Que, which he lovingly described to me.

One sort of fighting took place quite regularly, in which the Rhodesians took part. The other participants were members of 420 Squadron – a Canadian squadron which had recently arrived at Waddington, replacing the departed 207. At different times, both the Village Hall dances and the Horse and Jockey pub in the village were put out-of-bounds to one or both squadrons because of the ructions which tended to break out after a certain amount of alcohol had been consumed!

Eventually I was invited to the Horse and Jockey for a drink by Cecil. The Rhodesians had taken over the room known as the American Bar, at the far end of the pub, and we had to stumble along a blacked-out veranda at the back of the building to reach it. This caused difficulties for some at closing time! Still, we enjoyed a relaxed and happy evening among most of the Rhodesians I already knew, and an air-raid warning Red just as we were leaving didn't disturb us – though Cecil took my arm as we heard desynchronised engines above. They passed on, making for targets farther inland. I knew our ops would be taking off soon and I was on all-night duty; I'd be busy.

During this time, I was too occupied with my immediate circumstances and surroundings to take much notice of what was going on elsewhere, though I glanced through the occasional newspaper left in the Waafery rest-room or the NAAFI, and listened to the news on the radio. I knew we were after the *Scharnhorst* and the *Gneisenau*, which somehow seemed to give us the slip every time, and things weren't going too well for us in other theatres of the war either. There had been rumours of sabotage on the camp too, but it was difficult to know how believable they were. Like most, I never had any doubt that we'd win through eventually.

In the meantime, my thoughts were on more personal matters. There was an incident which disturbed and upset me. Going on duty one morning, I encountered groups of aircrew straggling back to MQ after de-briefing, all looking worn and strained. Among them were three I knew by sight as they lived in a house in a row opposite to my billet. One had his arm in a sling, and another, a foot heavily bandaged; he could only walk with the help of his crew-mates. I felt a surge of anger and compassion, seeing the hollow-eyed weariness in their faces. Couldn't anyone have provided transport – was that asking too much? I walked on helplessly, boiling inwardly at Authority's callousness in leaving them to walk the not inconsiderable distance from the Sergeants' Mess to their billet and a cold, cheerless room. Rita, a telephonist living downstairs in the billet I shared, caught up with me. She had passed them too, and was equally indignant. 'If I didn't have to go on duty, I'd have gone and lit a fire for them – even if I got jankers for being in their billet!' she said furiously.

Later in the afternoon when I was off duty, I saw one of the sergeants standing in the doorway of their house. On impulse, I went over to speak to him, quickly explaining that I and others from our billet had seen them that morning, and how angry we had been over the lack of transport, and I enquired how his crew mates were. He said they were OK, and only had flesh-wounds but wouldn't be flying again for a day or two; he was a little surprised at our concern over the transport – they had taken the situation for granted! Such maternal and protective instincts as I possessed were now thoroughly aroused. So were Rita's. We'd had a talk, and our thoughts ran along the same lines. I now offered them; perhaps we could help by doing the odd bit of ironing, mending or washing for them some time? Terry, as I later learned his name was, looked astonished, then a shy smile spread across his face. 'Oh – thanks!' he said. 'That's jolly good of you. I'll tell the others… um… if you really want to help, I know Dick, my pilot, has a shirt he has to iron – would you do that for him?' I asked for the shirt and Terry called Dick, who limped out and explained my offer to him. He was pathetically grateful. 'I never seem to be able to get the creases out when I do it – I don't like ironing,' he confessed. Removing the creases from a shirt seemed little enough to do after what I'd seen that morning.

From then on – for a while – we did these small domestic jobs for them. It was understood that no obligation existed either way, and it worked. Then the inevitable happened. I went on duty one morning and discovered they hadn't come back from the previous night's op. Well, that was how it was. We accepted it, shrugged, and said, 'That's that.' But underneath, we each had a nagging ache of sorrow.

Cecil gave me a shock. I saw him one evening after I'd been on night-duty and spent part of the day sleeping; I thought he looked tired, and commented on it. 'Well – it was a long night, and a cold one,' he said. I knew he would have been on duty at the flights and assumed this was what he meant, but he went on, 'particularly at 14,000 feet!' I stared at him, not instantly taking in what he had said because it was so unexpected. Then I reacted. 'No! Cecil, you weren't *flying*!'

'They took me along as spare gunner – it was a piece of cake!' he announced with satisfaction. I knew it hadn't been quite such a piece of cake – not all our aircraft had returned. I begged him not to take such a chance again, at least not until he had to. I could understand his urgent desire to find out what it was like since he was going to fly anyway, sooner or later, but I couldn't take the anxiety yet. He tried to reassure me, 'it's all right, kid, I'm here – nobody's shooting at me!' and explained that there probably wouldn't be another opportunity anyway. To further take my mind off the prospect he booked a dinner at the Horse and Jockey. My fears subsided. I hadn't visited the long, timbered dining-room before. It was light and warm and the meal luxurious by wartime standards. We had several drinks. Some of the other Rhodesians were there and greeted us, but tactfully did not join us. I was headily happy, and it wasn't the alcohol. I recognised the signs. I was falling in love again.

Cecil told me that the Rhodesians had organised a Christmas dance, to be held at the Assembly Rooms in Lincoln, and asked me to go with him. If I had to work half a dozen extra shifts in order to be off-duty for it, I would! He also confirmed the rumours I'd heard that 44 Squadron had been chosen as the first squadron in 5 Group to be re-equipped with the new heavy bombers: Lancasters. The air and ground crews were enthusiastic: none more so than the Rhodesians, as I realised watching Cecil's mobile features when he described what he'd seen and heard of the new aircraft. A prototype had already been demonstrated at Waddington, but I had missed seeing it. The Rhodesians were proud and happy, regarding it as something of a recognition of their services, and they were determined to surpass their previous reputation for keenness. Colonials they might be, but the 'Rooineks' had better watch out! Still, the Rooineks had their points – as was demonstrated on the way back from the H & J on that bitterly cold and frosty night.

On the other side of the airfield boundary hedge, on the road through camp, was a hut belonging to the RAF Regiment. Its tin chimney smoked in the cold air. 'Let's go in for a warm – they won't mind – I know them well,' Cecil suggested. Frozen, I followed him through the gap in the hedge. Inside, the hut glowed with warmth from a coke fire, red, crackling and spitting but incredibly welcoming. I was introduced to the occupants, to whom Cecil was obviously an old friend. They soon had the kettle on for mugs of tea, whilst we sat on a wooden bench thawing out. I warmed my hands round the steaming mug, beginning to feel drowsy, relaxed, happy and reluctant to leave. But we couldn't stay there indefinitely, and after we had finished our tea it was soon time to move on. The night glittered and sparkled like white fire in the light of the stars, but the beauty was too cold to linger over. My own cold room was unappealing and I didn't enjoy slipping out of my uniform and re-dressing in thick pyjamas, an old pullover and a pair of my father's socks, but it was the only way I could keep warm in bed – with my greatcoat over the blankets. I was no object of glamour on those chill nights.

Still, it had been a lovely evening I thought, hoping the sheets would soon warm up. I hoped there'd be more like it. In fact, a celebration was arranged when Cecil found out that my birthday was on December 16th – 'Dingaan's Day' in Rhodesia. I wasn't too sure whether I altogether liked the association since Dingaan was the treacherous brother of Chaka, the great Zulu chieftain!

My birthday gift from Cecil was a silver propelling pencil – something I could use every time I went on duty – and I treasured it. By now, I had ceased to be known as Phyllis. Cecil had re-christened me 'Pip' and I loved it. Oddly enough, it was a nickname I'd always coveted though the suggestion came from him – I had never mentioned it. The Rhodesians were fond of bestowing nicknames. Alec's girlfriend, a tiny, dark haired corporal with large brown eyes, was known as 'Tickey' – Rhodesian slang for a 3d piece – because of her diminutive size.

Three days before my birthday 44 Squadron mounted an operation of three aircraft – a daylight op. W/C Misselbrook, S/Ldr Burton-Gyles and Sgt Hackney were the pilots taking part in a 'Vegetable' of some importance – a minelaying trip to Brest, as I later learned. Sadly, W/C Misselbrook, 44's CO, was shot down. We were all shocked by the news. Sgt Hackney arrived back safely, and later, S/Ldr Burton-Gyles, who had first landed at an airfield on the south coast with extensive damage to his aircraft; he had also been attacked by fighters over the target.

On his return to Waddington, I saw him make a magnificent landing in his still crippled Hampden. He called up to say that he was going to attempt a one-wheel landing, as the other wheel would not come down. As he approached, we could see the aircraft had been badly shot up. The crash tender, ambulance and fire tender stood by, engines running, ready to race out at the earliest moment. In Control, the atmosphere grew unbearably tense as the Hampden drew closer; everyone stood silent, grimly waiting for the apparently inevitable crash. Down came the aircraft, a shattered wing tip now clearly visible, and then, touchdown. By a miraculous feat of control and balance, it sped along the runway on one wheel just as if a perfect three-point landing had been made.

The tension broke and there were shouts and cheers – everyone rushed out on to the balcony to see the end of the run. As the speed dropped the aircraft slewed gently round and came to rest, one wing tip scraping the ground. The ambulance and the two tenders drove out, but were not needed. 'Tell him "good show!"' the FCO instructed me – which I did enthusiastically.

The day of the Rhodesian dance arrived. I was off duty, and not on again until midday the following day – it could not have been better. Added to which, a notice appeared on SROs that morning to the effect that R/T operators were now entitled to wear the 'sparks' badge denoting a wireless trade. Not yet being officially qualified, it was highly questionable for me to wear one – but have one I must, if only for the dance. I took the somewhat irresponsible view that I was *going* to be an R/T operator, so I might as well have my badge anyway! I rushed off to Stores and drew one, sewing it on to my best blue with care; it looked very nice. I was going to be 'different' – one of the select band of WAAF sparks-wearers. I also wore the forbidden silk stockings – and, on my tie, the gold Rhodesian wings-badge which Cecil had given me. My hair I piled up in curls above my forehead – the most feminine style I could think of.

The transports picked up a high-spirited crowd outside the

Airmen's Mess that evening, Cecil and I included. The ballroom of Lincoln's Assembly Rooms was bright and festive, adorned with evergreens, balloons and paper streamers and, over the rostrum, 44's magnificent Elephant Crest draped with flags. A large bar led off the hall nearby. In no time, the whole place was full, the band playing and everyone dancing. We didn't miss a dance, except to stop for a much needed drink occasionally, until halfway through the evening when Cecil and some of the others had arranged to take over from the band; they were to play a selection of Rhodesian and South African tunes and songs. Cecil was playing the drums, for which he had a particular talent.

I planned to sit and listen, but instead was swept into the throng of dancers before I could protest by a sergeant-pilot who seemed to know me. He energetically danced me round to the bar entrance and into the bar. A drink was thrust into my hand and he proceeded to pay me ridiculously extravagant compliments, then tried to persuade me to have another drink. I politely refused. I could hear the last strains of 'Sari Marais' dying away, and the applause, and knew Cecil would be looking for me. I tried to excuse myself and get away but the sergeant, a trifle drunk, caught my hand to detain me. At that moment Cecil appeared in the doorway, took in what was happening, and came over to detach me with a threatening glare at the sergeant. We left him contemplating his beer. 'I looked all over for you!' said Cecil, looking as though he thought I might have gone home. We slid into the dancers again. The evening was in full swing, and from somewhere bottles of champagne suddenly appeared. Cecil fought his way through the press surrounding the nearest bottle and returned triumphant, bearing a glass for me. I'd never tasted champagne before, and expected something ambrosial; this was rather like bubbly cider, I thought – but still – one didn't have the opportunity to drink champagne every day. 'Mmm – lovely!' I said, ignoring a slight sense of disappointment.

The streamers and balloons were released, and everyone was draped in the multi-coloured paper swirls. The hall resounded to the popping of hundreds of balloons – a shame, I thought, they had looked so pretty! Some local press photographers arrived and we were all herded to one end of the hall whilst the cameras flashed, then the dance continued, by now fast and furious. Cecil and I went out into the foyer to cool off a little, sitting side by side on a velvet settee and holding hands; tired, but completely happy. Yes – I was in love. I knew it. I glowed.

From this time on, my perceptions heightened – everything came into sharper focus. I was vividly aware of the sunlight on snow or frost, delighting in every glittering crystal; sunsets gilding massing clouds of red or purple; first stars in a sky of clear blue-green; and the moon flooding cool white light over the airfield, making silver highlights and long black shadows. If this was love, it was wonderful. A mystical experience was born from my emotional state. I was walking down the main road of the camp, which seemed unusually deserted, gazing at a particularly gorgeous sunset and trying to absorb that glorious concentration of colour and light. With some surprise, I became aware of a pearly glow suffusing everything about me, and then I seemed no longer to be on the road but drifting high to the golden heart of the sunset, experiencing a feeling of great peace and tranquillity and an overwhelming sense of happiness. Suddenly it was over. The sun dipped below the horizon and I was back on the road again. Did I ever really leave it? I didn't know and couldn't explain it, but was full of wonder.

Sometimes on an off-duty afternoon, I walked along to the dispersal where Cecil worked on Hampden KM-D, D-Dopey the crew called it, as Cecil had painted Dopey of Seven Dwarfs fame on the nose; something else he had a flair for. It was very cold there, off the road which led on to FMU, and I didn't envy the ground staff. I never stayed long, mainly because Chiefy – the Flight Sergeant – would have come storming over to speed me on my way, and Cecil would have been in trouble for stopping work to talk to me. We sat together in the cookhouse. If sometimes it was too cold to go anywhere else, we went to George's, a ramshackle little café just outside No. 2 barrier and quite close to MQ. There, perched on high stools, over coffee and cream buns, we talked about our plans for the future. He wanted to marry me. 'But not until the war is over,' he stipulated. 'Things are too unsettled now and I don't want to tie you down, much as I want you to belong to me.' I was content to wait. He wanted me to have a ring, which delighted me, and I chose my birthstone – a lovely, oval turquoise in a plain gold setting. As he slipped it on to my finger he said, suddenly anxious, 'Pip – we *will* be married, won't we?' Wondering at his doubt, I answered, 'But you *know* we will!'

On Christmas Eve 1941, 44's first Lancasters arrived – a magnificent Christmas present for the squadron. It was with intense interest that everyone in Flying Control watched their approach and landing. As the first of the three taxied round the perimeter to the Watch Office, I stared in astonishment at this formidable and beautiful aircraft, cockpit as high as the balcony on which I stood and great spread of wings with four enormous engines. Its lines were sleek and graceful, yet there was an awesome feeling of power about it. It looked so right after the clumsiness of the Manchester, from which its design had evolved. Their arrival meant a new programme of training for the air and ground crews and no operations until the crews had done their share of circuits, bumps and cross-countries and thoroughly familiarised themselves with the Lancasters. There were one or two minor accidents at this time; changing from a twin-engined aircraft to a heavier one with four engines must have presented *some* difficulties – but the crews took to them rapidly. I heard nothing but praise for the Lancs.

On December 25th the officers donned aprons and served the erks with their Christmas dinner in the time-honoured custom. I wondered what they *really* felt about it. Cecil had a food parcel from home containing all sorts of good things, including a gorgeous rich fruitcake. He decided to have a party, since discipline was somewhat relaxed for Christmas Day. In WAAF billets, no one lived in the kitchen, which was where Cecil had made his home. He liked his privacy, but for tonight had made it warm and comfortable for us all. An old-fashioned round brick wash-boiler with fire-grate underneath glowed with heat. The kitchen tap provided water for washing-up and tea-making. His made-up bed and some borrowed chairs made up the seating arrangements. We fell on the contents of the food parcel with great enjoyment and appreciation, demolishing the rich tinned soup, tinned ham and sweetcorn served on toast – and, of course, the fruitcake and some chocolate. It was all delicious. The only thing not available was alcohol, but I don't think we noticed; our spirits were high enough anyway! Coats, caps and tunics were piled in a corner – the small room grew hotter and talk and laughter flowed. Alec had not yet put in an appearance. Suddenly the door burst open and he rushed in, bringing a draught of cold air and a warning: 'The Duty Officer and some SPs are just setting off to make an inspection of the billets – I let the air out of their car tyres outside the Guard Room to delay them a bit and ran!' At this dramatic announcement, we WAAFs gathered up our belongings and hastily departed to our own billets. There had evidently been second thoughts about the relaxation of discipline – or hopes of catching out occupants of MQ indulging in Christmas orgies!

Thoughtfully, Cecil's Christmas gift to me was an electric iron, plus more hoarded chocolate. The iron solved my washing problems by relieving me of the necessity of queuing for the use of Waafery irons, or borrowing Cecil's own.

The winter of 1941–42 was viciously cold. Sometimes it seemed as if the bitter east wind would never stop blowing, and I railed aloud and quite futilely at it as I trailed across the airfield convinced that I was being dissected by a thousand icy knives. The wind found its way through every crack and cranny of the Control Room windows; despite central heating, I was still cold, especially my feet. Dear Cecil! He produced a pair of flying boots from somewhere for me to wear on duty. There was room for me to put on my father's socks inside them too, and at last my feet were warm. If it was still dark when I came off duty, I kept them on to walk back, and clutched the hot-water bottle I had just filled, holding its comforting warmth close to me under my greatcoat. On reaching the billet, it went into my bed to warm icy sheets. At these times, the coal ration for our house was often used up too soon. Shift workers tended to use more coal than day workers as the occupants were off-duty at different times. There would be two, perhaps three days, without fuel. When this situation arose, regrettably one or more of us stole out after dark, taking a bucket, to see if we could locate a billet with a reasonable amount of coal in the outdoor shed. We then helped ourselves to enough to make a fire for a few hours. Visits which I am sure were reciprocated all round. Blessed was the day of coal delivery!

Snow blanketed the airfield and blew into great drifts. It was very beautiful to look out on from the Control Room, wearing my loaned flying boots – but less enjoyable to walk through when the blizzard raged. When it stopped all hands were called out to help clear the runways, and it was an amazing sight to see hundreds of airmen, aircrew and some WAAFs shovelling away until well into the dusk to free the main runway. Between the efforts of the snowploughs and the toiling shovellers, piles of snow lay by the sides of the runway and the job was done.

A little flying took place, and two of the precious Lancs suffered a small amount of damage, though not serious, in spite of the dreadful weather conditions. A different story to a pre-Christmas spell of bad weather, when fog suddenly descended just as the Hampdens operating that night were due to return. Most opted to try landing at Waddington rather than be diverted to another base. When I made my way to the Watch Office the following morning I was horrified to see Hampden tails sticking up through the fog all over the place – even one in front of the Sergeants' Mess! Yet astonishingly, there had been few serious injuries amongst the crews.

The weather eased up a little, and one day the airfield seemed to be overrun with boys from the Lincoln Air Training Corps. I watched enviously as they had trips in a Lancaster. If they could have this marvellous opportunity, why couldn't I? It was expressly forbidden for WAAF to go up in operational aircraft. The boys were wildly enthusiastic, of course, and though Cecil grumbled about them getting under everyone's feet, I suspected that he secretly sympathised with them. I suppose I did too. Towards the end of January 1942 I had a leave due. It seemed unthinkable that I should go home alone; Cecil managed to flannel a leave at the same time – we could hardly believe our luck. Nine whole days to be together.

Cecil had brought some 'civvies' with him and wore flannels and a shirt and tweed jacket – the first time I had seen him out of uniform. We put away our uniforms, forgot the war, and lived for the day – for the hour even – putting all else from our minds. I walked proudly beside him, noting the curious and interested stares of the Buckingham people who knew me, and probably still thought of me as little more than a schoolgirl. We went for long rambles in the surrounding countryside which I loved. I took him to Stowe Avenue and we walked the length of it to the Corinthian Arch; through it, over fields and lawns. The facade of Stowe School was visible with its warm stone, great portico, and Corinthian and Ionic pillars encircled by arms of still-leafless trees. Something out of a dream, it seemed, and we visited Oxford one day. I wanted to show Cecil all the places I was happy in, and this ancient city with lovely and gracious college buildings, river, and trees was very dear to my heart.

On our last evening there was to be a dance at the Town Hall – not just the usual weekly 'hop', but a dress occasion. We were going, of course. For Cecil it was back to uniform, but I could wear evening dress – my full-skirted taffeta in deep red and white – and a gold chain about my neck as my only jewellery, except for my turquoise ring. We had a heavenly evening, dancing only with each other. The turning, faceted globe suspended from the ceiling, spangled us with glitter, like stardust. The evening passed like a dream. The whole of our leave seemed dreamlike – and now it was over.

Within a few hours we were on the train going back to Waddington. The inevitable switch began to take place and we wondered what changes we'd find. Cecil was again concerned about the well-being of KM-D Dopey. Camp atmosphere claimed us long before we reached Lincoln, and we were almost eager to resume what had become to us a normal way of life. Our leave had become an interval out of time. An unpleasant shock awaited me. I was to be posted to Swinderby. It just couldn't happen; I begged the SFCO to get it cancelled if it were possible. He wasn't sure if he could. For days I lived on a knife-edge, not knowing if I was going or staying. Finally news came; the posting was cancelled! The expression on my face was enough to tell Cecil, before I even spoke.

The R/T operators' Board came at last – long last – and we sat in a room in the Waafery over our papers. We all passed, and rejoiced. How very satisfying it was to be able to abandon the irritating prefix, u/t, and to know that we were now qualified even if still only ACW2 in rank. *Now* we could put up the 'sparks' badge knowing no WAAF authority had the power to make us remove it. It was queried by the admin staff, but SHQ Signals were adamant about our entitlement to wear our sparks now so there was no further argument. Despite this, we learned that some of the wireless operators deeply resented it, feeling that our training was neither so long nor so concentrated as theirs. However, 'sparks' denoted a wireless trade rather than a specific job, so the W/Ops had perforce to accept it.

WAAF officers had no dominion over us in Flying Control and were not encouraged to visit the Watch Office over WAAF concerns; it was rare indeed to see one there. They did, of course, supervise most other aspects of our life on camp. As in Domestic Night – one night a week when all the WAAF Section not on duty was confined to camp and expected to do mending and other domestic chores. During the evening a WAAF officer, accompanied by one of the Admin staff, would inspect the billets and want to know the whereabouts of any WAAF who was not present. We resented Domestic Night. After all, we had time to do our mending at other times convenient to us, and quarters were inspected every morning. The general belief was that it gave the admin people something to do. Kit inspections took place from time to time, with the frantic borrowing attendant on the occasion. Missing items of kit were begged from friends on duty, with the fervent hope that a different name and number would not be noticed. Beds were stacked in the approved fashion and all kit displayed as required, in a clean and tidy condition; we stood by our beds quaking inwardly, unless fortunate enough to have a complete and unblemished array.

Whenever possible I got out of parades, which I detested. I suppose Pay Parade was the only one I didn't make strenuous efforts to avoid. Shift workers had a definite advantage when it came to either being on duty, or sleeping after night duty. In the morning, knowing that an inspection would take place around 11.00 hrs, we could put a notice on our door saying, 'Please do not disturb. Sleeping after night duty', which gave us considerable satisfaction. Of course, we had to be in bed; sometimes the door would open gently and we knew someone was checking that we really were sleeping. Periodically, FFI inspections were carried out – 'Free From Infection' – at WAAF Sick Quarters. This was a basic medical inspection of skin and hair to make sure we were clean and free of lice! We hated it, but appreciated it as a necessary precaution – a protection for the majority.

We felt Gas Drill too, to be a necessary evil. Gas masks and steel helmets were carried at all times, and to walk behind a row of WAAF complete with respirators and tin hats was to be reminded of a line of trees in a prevailing wind – all bowed to one side with the weight of the kit. We expected to become permanently tilted (a sideways Grecian bend), until some time later, and greatly to our relief, the rule on carrying tin hats was cancelled.

Gas Drill was held in a small hut behind No 1 hangar, and the procedure was for a number of us to be shut inside after a capsule of tear gas had been broken. We wore our respirators, and if anyone felt stinging eyes or was aware of the choking smell, they were unlucky. They had a leaky mask. After a few minutes of this we filed out, removed gas masks, and entered again, one at a time. This ensured that there'd be no doubts in our minds if we were ever unfortunate enough to encounter the gas in reality. The possibility was not one we cared to consider. After my first experience of the Gas Hut and the mild but unpleasant effects of a whiff of tear gas, I decided the best method of coping with the drill was to take a deep breath before entering, hold it, and once inside close my eyes and rush round and out as quickly as possible. This way the effects were minimal.

A PT session was held twice a week, a WAAF officer officiating. One afternoon was compulsory. I usually managed that. There was an occasion when I turned out to be the only participant and hopefully thought I'd be dismissed. But no – the WAAF officer and I touched toes, swivelled waists and circled ankles at each other for a whole half-hour. I took a dim view. Still – I thought my job was perhaps rather sedentary and it might be a good idea to do more about exercise – so I joined the station netball team. I went to some practices and played a couple of games – which we lost. 'Was it me' I wondered. Some of the best players were posted, and the depleted team ceased to exist. So ended my only venture into the world of sport. I wasn't particularly sorry. After all, I now had my bike, recently sent from home; I bowled happily around the camp and its environs, sometimes taking a trip to Lincoln on it. Bracebridge Hill was marvellous to swoop down, but the return journey was a different matter. 'Good exercise,' I thought – 'Good exercise!' as I toiled up it.

The Rhodesians' sport was rugger, and Cecil belonged to the team. If I happened to be off duty when matches took place, I was a spectator, though I knew less than nothing about the game. Efforts had been made to instruct me in the niceties of play, but to me it remained an exceedingly rough exercise in which groups of men occasionally lurched around in crab-like masses until a ball emerged mysteriously from their midst. After one game he invited me to accompany him to the tea held in the NAAFI in honour of the visiting team. I was abashed to find myself the only girl there. No one seemed to mind though, and it was a very much better tea than we would have had in the Mess! There were plenty of good-natured insults flying between the teams as we ate. Bruises blossomed and cuts swelled, but everyone was happy, and the occasion ended with each of the team captains making complimentary speeches about the other side. There were no rugger songs. All I had heard was what I took to be the Rhodesians' war-cry and song of encouragement to their own players:

> *Mow him down, the Swazi warrior,*
> *Mow him down, the Reds and Whites!*

Occasionally, WAAF DDs – the Daily Details which were placed on the Waafery notice board – decreed that someone's billet would be changed. Applications to share a room with friends were granted if possible, so the powers-that-be were not unfeeling. Thus, I found one morning that I was to move into a two-bed room with Pattie, a woman I knew only by sight. I was anxious about the change as she had a reputation of being sharp tongued and difficult to get on with. Older than most, she had a daughter in the ATS, whose photo was in a frame by her bedside. I took my kit along to her room, and we greeted each other guardedly. If there were only two of us together in the small room, we needed to get on or the atmosphere could be very uncomfortable.

As it turned out, we took to each other. The age difference proved to be no barrier, and perhaps worked in our favour; I, as a substitute daughter, she as someone I could talk to more easily than most older women because of our shared service experience.

Later, she told me she was glad we were sharing a room; she had feared she'd get some noisy careless type. But she found me easy to get on with and hoped I'd stay. I shared her wish – this feminine relationship was very good for me. I knew plenty of girls on the camp but as yet, had no real friends. I hadn't needed any because I had Cecil.

Early in March eight of 44's Lancasters were ordered to Lossiemouth, Cecil's aircraft among them. He expected to be away for about a week, depending on weather and other factors. The ground crews usually travelled by train, along with spares and equipment, but Cecil had succeeded in 'flannelling' a trip in the aircraft. He was looking forward to his first flight of any duration in a Lancaster. It had been quite an experience, he told me later. The Navy, in the shape of a convoy escort, had fired at them as they flew over it; a Spitfire next attacked the Lancs until frantic firing of the colours of the day convinced its pilot that they were not enemy aircraft. Luckily no damage or casualties had resulted beyond irritated and indignant aircrew. 'Oh well – the bloody Navy doesn't know its aircraft from its elbow!' But they had expected better from their own Service. If words could kill, the Spitfire would have gone down in flames.

4

Daylight to Augsburg

We had some excitement of our own at Waddington. It came on a grey cloudy day with no flying in progress – the airfield seemed deserted; not surprisingly since we had just had an air-raid warning 'red'. Suddenly out of the clouds streaked a fighter with another on his tail. In a moment all the Control staff were out on the balcony, and the Met Office occupants and the Flare Party appeared below, to watch the battle taking place scarcely beyond the boundary of the airfield. The two fighters twisted and rolled about each other, each feverishly trying to gain an advantage, and we heard the sharp stutter of machine guns. It was impossible to pick out which aircraft was ours. A sudden red glow of fire appeared in the fuselage of one, and grew rapidly, smoke pouring from it. A cheer broke out from the watchers; it could only be the enemy! Slowly the burning aircraft spiralled down, trailing dense black smoke. We didn't see it hit the ground and explode, but heard it, and then watched the low cloud redden in the glow of its burning. The victor circled his kill and departed. Afterwards we heard that he was the pilot of a Beaufighter from our neighbouring fighter station, Coleby Grange. We went inside elated at our victory. It was the first dogfight many of us had witnessed. I suppose we all privately shared the shudder of horror at the thought of a human body trapped in the flames. I hoped he died from bullets rather than fire. But there was more fire a few nights later.

It was dark and quiet outside. What flying there was had been completed. It was quiet, with half of 44's aircraft still away. All of us in Control were peacefully following our own occupations when the R/T broke into life: a 'Darky' call. 'Darky' was a codeword conveying that an aircraft was lost or in urgent need of assistance.

'Hello Darky, hello Darky, Lino C-Charlie calling, may we land?' 'Hello Lino C-Charlie, this is Waddington. Prepare to land,' I replied, whilst the Control Officer switched on the airfield lighting and alerted the Crash Crew and Sick Quarters.

'Hello Waddington, I am coming in, I have one engine u/s.' The voice sounded strained and anxious.

In the meantime, Mr Cabourne, the recorder, had identified the call sign. 'From an OTU,' he observed. 'Get in touch with them,' ordered Hobby, the FCO. We heard the aircraft roar over the airfield. 'It's a Wimpy,' called someone watching from the balcony.

The chance light was on, blazing down the runway. Again the plane swept over low.

'Give him another call,' the FCO instructed.

'Hello Lino C-Charlie, Waddington here, are you in trouble?' A silly question – of course he was in trouble, but was there anything more we could do? We waited. The reply was not immediate. Then, 'Hello Waddington, yes, I can't...' and the sentence trailed off as though every last shred of concentration was needed in holding the Wimpy's controls. I gave him a moment and called again, but there was no reply. Those last few words from the pilot had been high-pitched, frantic. We heard the engines approaching again, and Hobby told me to try another call. I did, but the R/T remained silent. Then the Wimpy shot out of the night, very low over the runway, and before anyone could even move there came a dreadful, rending crash from the direction of Green Lane, and a great rush of flame spurted from the broken aircraft.

The crash crew, fire tender and ambulance were already on their way to the crash, and Hobby followed in the Utility. He was soon back. 'Poor devils crashed near the sewage plant,' he said. 'No one could get near. No survivors.' Matter-of-factly, he added, 'I suppose, being inexperienced, he panicked a bit and turned in on his duff side and stalled.' I felt shaken and sick. It had all happened in moments, and in that short space five young men had died in the smoking pyre of their aircraft; mine had been the last voice they had heard – would ever hear. I felt related to them in a strange hollow intimacy; the experience haunted my dreams for a while. I didn't know then, and it wouldn't have made any difference to my feelings if I had, that in RAF statistics this was a commonplace little tragedy.

44's Lancasters returned from Lossiemouth – Cecil was back and the world seemed complete again. He brought me a tartan needlecase as a souvenir, and we had much to tell each other. Cecil liked to keep me up to date with information about our aircraft, which he knew I soaked up with keen interest; thus it was that I came to possess samples of leaflets extracted from bundles loaded up for dropping over France and Germany in early 'Nickel' raids. Likewise, pieces of 'Window' – strips of metal foil which were to be dropped from our aircraft to confuse enemy radar. Except that it had not yet been used, and was not to be until the following year though we were not aware of it then.

Visiting the dispersal where he worked one day, I noticed on a neighbouring hard-standing a Lancaster with different engines. 'They', I was told, 'are *radial* engines – it's a Mark II Lanc. Our Mark Is have *in-line* engines. The Mark IIs are Bristol Hercules Is, which as you know, are Merlins.' I was given some more technical detail, but that didn't stick. However, at least I could recognise a Lancaster with radial engines and say, knowledgeably, 'Ah yes – a Mark II – Bristol Hercules!' and feel rather smug.

I was introduced to IFF very early on by Joe and Mac in Flying Control, the system of 'Identification, Friend or Foe' being explained to me by them. Later, Cecil told me about the magic Gee box – all extremely hush-hush. There was a good deal of quiet excitement when the Lancasters were fitted with these. The men R/T operators were in the process of departing. Mac had been commissioned and was to become a Flying Control Officer; indeed, after his initial training he came back to us to gain further experience and we were pleased to see him back. Joe and Jock opted for further training in Signals, with a view to a commission, and Jack and Ken were both posted to the MEF. We were joined by Joan – another WAAF who had her exclusively-tailored uniform in officers' cloth; something not altogether approved of by WAAF officers, but there seemed to be nothing they could actually do about it. No doubt KRs had not got around to this particular situation! It was a while before I came to know Joan very well as we were on opposite shifts, so saw very little of each other. She was tall and rather thin, with light brown hair and large, liquid blue eyes which opened wide, exposing the pupils completely when she was surprised or upset; she talked quickly.

During April, a suspicion grew in Control that something big was being laid on for sometime in the near future, and 44 would not be the only squadron involved. There had been frequent visits from S/Ldr Sherwood and F/Lt Penman of 97 Squadron at nearby Woodhall Spa, who of course reported into Control at each landing, as all visiting aircraft were required to do. Cecil had also mentioned the low-level cross-country flight practices which were taking place, and we wondered what they presaged. On April 17th we found out.

I was on duty at 13.00 and found a daylight op was due to takeoff at 15.00 – six aircraft, led by S/Ldr Nettleton, whose co-pilot was Pat Dorehill, a friend of Cecil's and a fellow-Rhodesian. I had met him once, in Cecil's company. The names of the other pilots were all familiar to me since I saw them most days on the ops board; F/O Garwell, Sgt. Rhodes, F/Lt Sandford, and W/O's Crum and Beckett. Some I knew by sight, but none personally. There was still no mention of the target, which was unusual as it was generally an open secret well before takeoff. Perhaps the FCO knew – if so, he was saying nothing. The take-off proceeded normally, with little to show that it was any different from any other operational take-off. I had changed shifts with another operator so did not go on duty that night as would have been usual, but was instead doing morning and evening duties the day after. So it was not until the next morning that I learned of the terrible toll the raid had exacted. There was no way to express the horror that I, like everyone else on the station, felt. The whole camp seemed shocked and silent.

Twelve aircraft – six from 44 and six from 97 – had attacked the MAN factory at Augsburg, deep in Germany, successfully we were told, and with unbelievable courage. But of our six aircraft, S/Ldr Nettleton's was the only one to return; five did not – thirty-five men missing – thirty-five empty bunks, thirty-five empty places at the table, shared between the Officers' and the Sergeants' Messes. Many of us wondered if it was worth it.

We were proud of S/Ldr Nettleton's VC, immediately awarded – heaven knew he had earned it... but what of the others? Incredibly, as we learned much later, there were survivors, just a few. 97 had lost two Lancasters, but S/Ldr Sherwood, the pilot of one, lived, and made his way back to England a few weeks later. W/O Crum, from 44, had managed to crash-land his badly-damaged aircraft, but he and his crew were all eventually taken prisoner and spent the rest of the war as POWs At least they lived. But there were no medals for them.

Before the month was out, another trip to Lossiemouth was on, and six of 44 Squadron's aircraft flew off to Scotland. Cecil was again among the ground crew, and this time had to travel by train. He hated the long, dreary journey and would have much preferred the air trip despite the hazards of his previous flight up north. During his absence, an incident occurred which caused a certain amount of amusement in Control. We had several RFC veteran pilots as Flying Control Officers, and it was well known that one of them was itching to try his hand at flying again. Eventually he got permission to take up the Station Commander's precious Tiger Moth – not an easy favour to obtain. We watched him taxi out on to the perimeter track, a happy man.

Some distance ahead of him on the perimeter stood a Lancaster, revving up its engines. The Moth taxied on. Suddenly the Lancaster's revs increased; the little Moth caught the full force of the back-draught, and flipped neatly over, wheels spinning in air. The FCO switched off the engine but – a large man – he hung helplessly upside-down in his straps. The crash-crew hurried out to release him from his undignified position and turn the Moth upright; fortunately there was little damage to it. There was no question of another try – the Moth was towed back to the hangar to be checked over. The pilot walked sheepishly away. We truly sympathised with him in spite of our mirth. And the Lancaster? It taxied off apparently unaware of the little drama behind. Accidental? We wondered!

I had a come-uppance of my own. I longed for another trip with BAT Flight, so took the CO at his word and presented myself once more at his office. Yes – I could go up! The Squadron Leader would again take me in his own Oxford with his pupil-pilot. The formalities were gone through, and very soon we were in the aircraft and rolling down the runway. The tyres swished along, and then left the tarmac – and we were airborne. It was a rather grey afternoon; a high layer of greyish-white cloud obscured the sun and there were more clouds below, which the pupil passed through as he did his beam-practice.

I wasn't enjoying this as much as I should, I thought. Then, aware of a generalised discomfort which rapidly became local, I understood why. Remembering the earlier instruction, I urgently tapped the Squadron Leader on the shoulder and pointed downwards. He stuck up a thumb and started an immediate crescent. But oh! The shame of it! I turned away, and up came my lunch. I apologised profusely when we landed, and asked for something to clean up the mess with. 'Don't worry,' BAT Flight's CO said kindly, 'I'll get someone to clean up – never mind.' I did mind though, and knew I'd never be able to ask him for another flight, even though this was perhaps just an off-day. I walked off slowly and miserably.

A deep voice hailed me from inside an open door in the hangar: 'Come in and have a cup of tea – you look as though you're on your knees!' The owner of the voice was a wireless mechanic I knew by sight, but had not spoken to before. He introduced himself and said: 'Now – what's wrong?' I explained about the flight, though he had apparently already guessed what had happened, from my downcast manner. He sat me down and gave me a cup of tea, and chatted away to me until I felt better, and at least looked somewhat more cheerful than before. Tall, athletic, pipe-smoking James – he looked more like a young professor than a veteran of the International Brigade and the Spanish war, as I later discovered. James was a great character, and became a dear friend, but at that moment I was immensely grateful for his timely aid and comfort.

I was making a number of new friends and acquaintances. One of them was to become my closest friend – Sally Whelan. She was the station's first WAAF wireless operator, and so became as great a novelty in SHQ Signals as the R/T operators had been in Flying Control. Her brown-gold hair fell across her forehead in a deep wave; her eyes were large, blue, and guileless. But there was an innocent guile in the smile that lit her face – her tongue-tip protruded slightly between a small gap in her teeth caused by an irregularity in growth, of which she had been very conscious since girlhood, and had thus tried to disguise it. She had been surprised and puzzled to discover that men found it provocative. Her fair complexion had a scatter of golden freckles. She was the same height and build as I – small, slim, and rounded.

She told me how she had come to be posted to Waddington. Earlier, she had been at RAF Chivenor, in Devon. Then came a posting to Chicksands Priory, in Bedfordshire. Chicksands, she said, was all girls, girls, girls – lovely girls, too, she added. It was, or had been, a Priory, and the girls were transported from Wrest Park – a stately home taken over by the RAF – and where they were billeted in some splendour. They worked continuous night-duty, listening out for German broadcasts. Very little happened though – it was a rare occasion, Sally said, for anyone to hold up a piece of paper for the supervisor to rush along to the cypher office.

'Lots of outings were arranged for us, to make up for the night duties, and the seclusion,' she continued. She also said that it had never been known for anyone to be posted away from Chicksands. She enjoyed the gracious surroundings – the lake, with its water lilies and herons, and the pheasants walking around, quite unafraid of the girls. There was, she described, an imposing mausoleum in the grounds, with a flight of broad stone steps leading up to it on which the girls acted plays they would make up, or pretended to be eighteenth-century ladies with crinolines and piled-up hair; quite a feat of imagination, and all great fun. But it wasn't enough.

One thing Sally was unhappy about was not doing any transmitting, which she had been used to doing at Chivenor, and considered part of her job. The other thing was – well, no men! Somehow, she had to change things. Chicksands was part of Coastal Command. So, what to do? Why, write to Sir Philip Joubert, C in C of Coastal Command! She set out the facts – that she wasn't doing the job money had been spent on training her to do – no transmitting, only keeping a listening watch. She felt she could be much better employed on an operational station, using the experience she already had. 'I couldn't very well say to Sir Philip that there were no men, and I was afraid no one would ever ask me to marry them!' she added, laughing. Some time later, she was called in to see the WAAF officer. In her office, she saw her own letter on the desk together with another, typewritten letter, and quailed inwardly, wondering what was going to happen. In fact, not very much did, she said. She was told that she was to be posted, but not where. 'I don't think they'd ever come across anything like it before – a mere ACW, writing to such a superior superior!'

The other girls envied her, and looked on her as someone rather special, for being able to organise her own posting. On the day of her departure though, she suddenly felt very close to them all and didn't want to go, she admitted. But the posting was there. She could hardly turn it down! Just before she left, she was given her travel warrant and, glancing at it, thought her destination was 'Warrington'. Her heart sank. But a second look dispelled gloom – it was Waddington – an operational station! 'And the sun was shining beautifully!' she ended.

Another girl I met and liked was Doreen, but knew her less well. She told me something about herself though. She had married Terry Byrne, who was a W/Op AG in Lucky Wright's crew on 44 Squadron. She was puzzled and saddened because Lucky would not speak to her until the crew's tour (Terry's second) was completed. Then at last, he said he could hand Terry over to her. He hadn't approved of the marriage, fearing that it might interfere with Terry's concentration; it probably had the opposite effect, making him more careful and watchful than ever, since he now wanted to be as sure as humanly possible of returning to Doreen. With a tour on Hampdens with 83 Squadron behind him, he was no inexperienced boy. The pair were regarded by all who knew them as being the station's great romance. Doreen, who worked in Intelligence, carried everyone's good wishes as she walked by on Terry's arm, so tiny and vulnerable. We were glad he had finished with ops.

There was another marriage – a girl in my billet. This was Jean, who lived downstairs. Eighteen years old, 5 foot nothing, with a cloud of dark hair and dark eyes, a pale face and a sweet, husky little voice. Her favourite song-of-the-moment was 'Not a Cloud in the Sky', and we loved to hear her sing. Sitting by the fire in her room, one or other of us would beg her to sing it, and if she shyly demurred we would cry, 'Oh, go on!' She usually gave in, thinking no doubt of her Peter – Peter Rix, a Rhodesian in P/O Hackney's crew, as she crooned the romantic words.

After she returned from the short honeymoon leave they'd had, two of us from the billet sat talking to her, and one, unforgivably, asked, 'What was it like, Jean-you know!' Just as bad, I listened, all ears. 'Oh...' said Jean, embarrassed, 'Well, I – I don't know... I didn't like it very much. We didn't press for further details. Poor Jean – and poor Peter. In less than two months she had lost him. Flying with F/Sgt Tetley, he didn't come back from a trip to Dusseldorf. She was paler still, with dark rings around her eyes, and stunned. We never saw her cry. Neither did we hear her sing again.

Cecil had returned from Lossiemouth after a week's absence but now he was on detachment yet again, this time to Nutts Corner in Northern Ireland – for a whole month. It seemed interminable. We wrote every day, but if letters were held up in the post, as could happen for days on end, I was desolate. We seemed to have been apart so much. When at last he was back, we decided to do something about the situation, if possible. We were going to try for two weeks' leave together, and go home again. 'If you can make it, put two bricks on the roof of your coal house so I can see it first thing in the morning!' he ordered. We found we could both make it. He swung me round and round with joy at this discovery, both of us laughing with delight. And then – there had to be a then – his long-awaited posting to Aircrew Reception Centre came through, and on the day we had planned to travel to Buckingham, he was on his way to St. John's Wood. I was in tears – but there was nothing to be done. This, after all, was what he had come to England for – to become a pilot. So again we were separated. I went on leave, but it all seemed so flat and lonely. In the middle of the first week I decided, on the spur of the moment, to go to London and try to see Cecil. Apart from St. John's Wood, I had no idea where to look, as I hadn't yet got his address. However, I had some luck. The Aircrew Reception Centre was only a short distance from the tube station. I went in, found a sympathetic sergeant, and explained what I was trying to do. On checking, the sergeant told me where Cecil was billeted, pointing in the direction of a block of flats further down the road. Glancing at his watch, he said doubtfully: 'I don't know whether you'll find him there now though.' I thought I could at least walk along and enquire.

As I neared the entrance, three airmen with white flashes in their forage caps emerged; one of them was Cecil! He didn't see me immediately, being engaged in lively conversation with the other two. When he did, his face lit up. 'Pip!' he shouted. And like opposite poles of a magnet we were suddenly together, clinging, laughing, and kissing in the middle of the pavement.

When we had recovered our senses a little, Cecil introduced me to his companions, who had stood back surprised and smiling at our meeting. I didn't take in their names. They were all on their way to a lecture, but Cecil immediately decided to skip it, and said we would go and have some tea. So, arm-in-arm, we went off to Lyons Corner House, Piccadilly. Afterwards, I couldn't remember whether we walked or caught a bus or went by tube. It didn't matter; we were together. Even in my euphoric state, I couldn't avoid being aware of London's bomb damage. There were great gaps where buildings had been reduced to piles of rubble, and vast cellars open to the sky, with rough board fences around to prevent people falling into them in the blackout. London's ancient dust lay everywhere. I thought how terrifying it must have been for the occupants when this fearful devastation took place, and flames leapt up from the streets whilst searchlights flicked across the sky and ack-ack guns thudded. This I had seen on the newsreels. Now, seeing the results for myself, I was profoundly thankful the blitz wasn't something I'd had to live through. I wondered if I would have had the courage. But at that moment, I didn't think about it for too long.

After our meal, we decided to go to the cinema, where we enjoyed the long, double-feature programme; and perhaps more, just sitting together in the dark. The smoke from innumerable cigarettes swirled in the projector's flickering light above. People came and went, having reached the point in the programme where they came in. Back went the seats, as we stood up to let them pass, but we sat on. We came out with just enough time to dash round to good old Lyons for supper. I was booked in at the YWCA near Euston, and should have been in an hour ago. Cecil should also have been in billets. Who cared? He took me to Euston and saw me in, taking the blame for my lateness to the dragon who reluctantly answered my repeated rings on the bell. It was shattering to say goodbye again after those few, sweet hours. Cecil had said on our way back that he'd almost certainly be on a charge the next day, for either skipping a lecture or not being in billets on time – but it had been worth it.

It seemed pointless to stay on if I couldn't expect to see him. Also, I couldn't really afford it. I was still glowing with happiness though; we had had – was it eight hours? – together, and London had bloomed for us, even if only to our eyes. I went home feeling I couldn't have asked for more. Cecil wrote – he'd escaped being charged, and all was well. A friend had covered up for him at the lecture, and by impersonating the corporal-of-the-guard who luckily hadn't completed his rounds, he got back into his billet undetected; resourceful as ever. This was good news; being on a charge at that stage would not have been advantageous to his aircrew ambitions. If anything had gone wrong, I'd have felt it to be my fault for not considering it in advance – but I hadn't even thought about it. I hadn't thought of anything except seeing him.

I was almost glad when my leave was over and I was back in camp, though arriving in Lincoln alone and no one there to meet me wasn't a welcome experience. I missed Cecil dreadfully. A notice went up in the Waafery: plans were afoot to start a choral society. This appealed enormously to me. I adored music, and had started singing in my school choir, continuing in choral groups at home; surely it was just what I needed. A varied group of people turned up for the inaugural meeting – all from ground trades, since it wasn't the sort of interest aircrew would be likely to commit themselves to. No officers either – their absence making for a more relaxed atmosphere.

Corporal John Maxwell, a soft-spoken Scot, was the

organiser and choirmaster. He was a highly talented musician; an LRAM and occasional conductor of the Glasgow Orpheus Choir; we were incredibly lucky to have Mac, as he was soon universally and affectionately known. James, of BAT Flight, came with two friends, Shorty and Don. Tim, Jo, and Norman, a trio of flight mechanics, joined us, and John, an armourer. They, along with Sally, Joan (from Flying Control) and myself, formed the choir's nucleus. Others came later, but among the founder members, a bond of friendship formed which was to last many years.

We discussed our aims, and the sort of music we would try out, not yet knowing our potential. Perhaps some Bach and Handel... ballads... a few popular songs... yes, something for everybody. We would plan for a concert to be given on camp, and if we felt we were good enough, maybe in the surrounding villages later. Mac wanted us to sing some Scottish songs, and 'The Road to the Isles' and 'The Eriskay Love Lilt' were unanimously decided on. I hadn't come across the Love Lilt before, and was enchanted with its haunting cadences. Though I couldn't sight-read music, I quickly picked up the notes by ear, and was soon happily carolling away. Mac suggested that I should sing it as a solo, with the rest of the choir providing the chorus. 'Me?' I gaped at this suggestion. 'Well, don't look so surprised – you sing it very sweetly,' rejoined Mac. 'But I've never sung a solo in my life!' I protested. 'Then it's time you did – don't worry – you'll have plenty of time and lots of practice!'

Sometimes, in spite of my new-found interest, depression would catch up with me and then I sang quietly and just for myself, 'It's a Lovely Day Tomorrow', and 'With a Smile and a Song', in an effort to banish the blues. Singing was a great emotional release. The choir became, more than ever, a refuge for me. Cecil was posted to EFTS at Sywell, near Northampton. If only I'd known, and saved up my leave: we could easily have met in Northampton. But of course, there had been no way of knowing.

Flying Control and the choral society kept me going. The first of the thousand bomber raids had taken place, to be followed by two more, though it was some time after when we got to know of these momentous operations. We only knew of our own station's ops. The wider implications generally escaped us. I still adored my job, and when it was quiet – well, there were always letters to answer. My correspondence list seemed to grow longer. As well as my daily letters to Cecil and frequent missives to my parents, I wrote to numerous servicemen: boys who had joined up from Buckingham; friends of other people's boyfriends who wanted someone from home to write to; sons of my mother's friends from Canada or Australia or New Zealand who were now in other parts of the globe – just friendly letters or aerogrammes, written on a special form supplied by post offices. This was handed in and then photographed and reduced in size, to be as light as possible for airmail. I hoped the people who received these could read my writing; I had my doubts.

I loved receiving letters – and answering. Hitching into Lincoln one day, a sailor gave me a lift on the back of his motorbike – and asked me to write to him, as he was just going to sea. I agreed, but after a while his letters grew so sentimental that I stopped writing. Only one person could send me letters like that; and he was now in Cornwall – farther away than ever. I added studying French grammar to my quiet duty periods. Off duty, the choir became a way of life. Sometimes, Mac played for us after we had finished our practice – Mozart, Chopin, Bach. He sat at the piano absorbed in the music, a cigarette in his mouth, ash forming on it, forgotten, whilst the magic in his fingers held us spellbound. As we got to know each other better, any small group of us not on duty often went out together. Concerts were very popular; being in uniform gave us the benefit of reduced or free entry, often to hear performances by famous musicians, and a new world began to open for me. It was a totally different experience to radio listening, and one I had never met before. The powerful emotions created by the combination of music and the artistry of the musician in the atmosphere of a concert hall was exciting and exhilarating; sometimes soothing, often joyous. We all loved it. I was immersed in music, expanding into it.

We had tea in Lincoln, sometimes at Boots' cafe over the shop, which had a small 'Palm Court' orchestra – usually three elderly ladies and a male pianist playing light classics or tunes from operetta; a pleasing background to our talk and laughter. Once, there on my own, a lady sharing the table chatted to me and ended by inviting me to visit her. She told me that several other servicemen and women came to her house. I went one evening. An airman was there, and she gave us sandwiches and tea, whilst he and I talked of T S Eliot and Christopher Isherwood, feeling very intellectual and literary. Not that we really understood much of either, but the words reached out to us. I visited the hospitable lady once or twice more, but choir commitments and duties caught up with me, and I didn't go again, but never forgot her kindness. On my own by choice, I went to the cinema to see *For Whom the Bell Tolls*. I had read Ernest Hemingway's book, finishing it one night duty with tears streaming down my face and hoping no one would notice. Seeing the film was much worse – I emerged with red eyes and a sodden hanky, sniffing – though in this, I wasn't alone.

My tears came more easily, fuelled by the longing to see Cecil again. When could I hope for that, I wondered – and then thought guiltily about Pat in Flying Control, and her POW fiancé. Did she cry herself to sleep every night? How awful, not to know if she would ever see him again, not even be able to communicate properly, and then I was almost in tears for her plight. Perhaps going to see the film hadn't been such a good idea after all.

I tried a short spell of evening classes in Lincoln. Jo, who was an architect in civilian life, asked me if I would like to go to Art classes with him. I had enjoyed drawing and painting since childhood though didn't think I had any great talent – but it would be interesting to have professional tuition. We decided on life classes – or at least, Jo did. I went along wondering if I'd find it terribly embarrassing; I needn't have concerned myself – the model wore a bathing costume! I gave up my attendance after a while, for the inevitable reason. I missed so many classes through duty or the choir. I should have known, of course; though I had enjoyed the atmosphere of the classes in that dignified old building of warm red brick, mantled with Virginia creeper. And I'd always had a yen to go to Art School.

There was much that I enjoyed about Lincoln. I found I

wholeheartedly approved of my birthplace. Not that I could remember anything of the early years – but yes – I'd done well to choose this city! Nothing could be more beautiful than the cathedral. It stood high and serene, a landmark for miles around, and nothing could destroy it. To walk along the High Street to the Stonebow, and beyond to Steep Hill with the welcome iron handrail to help climbers ascend. Then along the even steeper Straight, passing little mediaeval houses, emerging breathless into the Cathedral Close. Then the final reward; there, all the splendour and delicacy of carved stone: The magnificent arches of the West Front and the sculptured frieze – the soaring towers, pinnacled at each corner – grace and grandeur against a changing sky.

In the cool dim interior, all was peace and silence, and the little buzz of people became insignificant. Religion had slipped away from me, but there was something here, more than beauty, which was all around. Perhaps an atmosphere of healing and reassurance, or perhaps something different for everyone. I didn't know; but I always felt refreshed when I came away. I seized the rare opportunity to attend a service, for the utter joy of listening to the choir. A clear treble solo soaring to the heights of the arched roof and becoming hushed in the misty darkness, joined then by the richer notes of the tenors, baritones and bass voices, seemed to vibrate through my body and shimmer along my nerves in an intensity of feeling.

Bodily refreshment was also obtainable in the vicinity – a WVS canteen in the august surroundings of the Bishop's Palace. We called it, familiarly, The Bishop's Pal, and those of us who went there loved it. The rowdier element kept away, and it was quiet, comfortable and gracious, with chintzy armchairs and polished tables and vases of flowers. The WVS ladies provided us with good, home-baked scones and tarts, cakes, and tea. It was a haven in which to read, write, talk, or just sit and laze. A lawn at the back sloped down to a stone wall at the edge of the cathedral cliff, and the rooftops of Lincoln spread away below. Once, feeling energetic, I walked all the way from Waddington to Lincoln, and up the hill to the Bishop's Pal, longing for a cup of tea. This I had, and a couple of jam tarts, taking cup and plate out on to the lawn in the sun. When I ate the tarts, I thought I had never tasted anything so good; I wasn't sure what the jam was, but it was like the essence of summer. I stretched out on the grass, the grey stone Palace behind me and the towers of the cathedral above, and felt absolutely content.

One warm, golden evening, Sally and I went into Lincoln with Tim and Jo. The boys suggested taking out a boat on the river and we agreed enthusiastically. So, to Brayford Pool we went, and hired a boat. Tim and Jo took turns in rowing and we made leisurely progress for quite a distance. It was very soothing to listen to the splash of the oars and watch the sun making rainbows in the water droplets as the oars were raised. We trailed our hands in the ripples spreading around us. The surface of the river looked like liquid gold; it was a glorious evening, and undoubtedly this was a pleasure to be repeated. The warm weather held, and several evenings later, I was in Lincoln again with Sally. We considered taking out a boat ourselves. Neither of us had rowed before but it didn't look too difficult, and it would be cool and peaceful on the river. It didn't occur to us to exercise much care in the choice of our craft. We took what we were given – a queer little tub that was almost triangular in shape and, we soon found, which seemed to have a mind of its own.

I took the oars, intending to get well out into the middle of the river, and Sally took the rudder. Somehow things were not going properly. The boat lurched drunkenly from side to side, and rowing was much harder than I'd anticipated; the oars slithered about in the rowlocks and didn't come cleanly out of the water like they did when Tim or Jo rowed – what was *wrong*? 'Jiggle the rudder about a bit more,' I suggested, and Sally did, but it only seemed to make matters worse. Still – having got this far, we intended to keep trying; after all, we couldn't expect to get the hang of it instantly. So we continued our zigzag progress, if that was the right word. Once or twice, we turned a complete circle in the middle of the river, which was interesting. Our erratic course didn't go unnoticed from the banks. Small boys shouted at us. Sailors and soldiers and airmen standing on bridges, cheered us, and shouted advice. 'Left – left a bit –

steady!' Steady? We collapsed into helpless giggles, completely lost control of our boat (if we'd ever had any) and rammed the riverbank; there we remained until we had got our breath back.

We thought it wise to turn round at this stage, and Sally took the oars – with no more success than I'd had. I was no better with the rudder either. On attempting to get away from the bank, we shot across the water and rammed a tethered barge, which caused our boat to turn sharply and almost hit a passing craft clearly under much better control than ours. The occupants snarled at us. Once more we were helpless with laughter. I began to get anxious about our return – could we make it? Somehow we did. Somehow we hit (literally) the right landing stage. The proprietor looked at us; we looked at him. Nobody said anything. Probably none of us dared. We decided to leave rowing to the boys in future.

The choral society expanded into a dramatic society as well, and our membership increased. We gained two members from the professional stage – Frank and Jan. Jan's mother was French, and he was lean and dark, with Gallic good looks. He showed us photos of Cannes, where he used to holiday pre-war... he was very unsuitably employed in Stores as an equipment assistant, and hated it. Frank was a wireless operator, which he enjoyed. Plays were discussed, thought about, turned down. Finally, we settled on 'Rebecca'. Instantly there was silent rivalry between Sally and myself as to who should get the main part. Both of us were secretly determined to have it, having seen the film. We could each envisage ourselves as the simple, shy heroine – playing opposite Laurence Olivier preferably – but failing him, well, whoever was cast would do! The choice fell on Sally. I was to be the dark, sinister Mrs Danvers.

But in fact we never produced the play, as a key member of the cast was posted and we had no one suitable to replace him. Our next effort was a concert with mainly musical items. One of them was a dance routine in which Jan and I would dance to variations in rhythm on the tune, 'Dancing in the Dark'. Jan choreographed it, and more coaching lessons in the Waafery ensued; he was marvellously patient. My only previous dancing experience was of the usual ballroom variety, and though I loved it I felt like a baby elephant as we practised the routines he had devised. But confidence came as I grew more accustomed to the steps, and finally my performance met with Jan's approval.

Another play was considered, and we started to read 'The Importance Of Being Earnest' and thought for a while we might produce this. I was even cast as Gwendoline. But again conditions went against us, and it was abandoned. Still – the concert party plans were progressing, and we had obtained permission to use the Gym as our theatre.

Then came the night of our first performance. The dress I should have worn for my dance had not arrived, though I had written to ask my mother to send it some time previously, and received her reply saying she had posted it. I was in a dreadful panic. Joan came to the rescue with the offer of an evening dress. She was a little taller than I, and I was terrified that I would trip over the swirling folds of the deep blue skirt as I danced. However, there was no time to try it out. In the event, I had no difficulty, dancing mostly on my toes with the hem swinging just clear of the floor. It was enough concentrating on my steps and the whispered instructions from Jan – whom I hadn't told of my dress problems – but in spite of all, I enjoyed my dancing debut, and we were clapped enthusiastically.

Mac played the piano solos superbly, and the choir sang the songs he had taught us. I sang 'The Eriskay Love Lilt', absolutely quaking. The choir hummed a counter-melody behind me, making a mist of music as Mac had intended, and it went well. Our audience was respectable in size, and seemed to appreciate our efforts if the applause at the end was anything to go by. I decided that being applauded was pleasant. We were all a little light-headed with relief at our success – we hadn't known what to expect. I described it all in detail in my next letter to Cecil, and had a quick reply. He was delighted that it had gone so well – wished he could have been there to see me and hear me sing – *but* – he was hoping to get leave soon! I instantly forgot about applause, success, anything – just that we'd be together again. That evening, I poured out all my joyful anticipation to Pattie. She listened silently and said finally, when I looked at her in surprise for her lack of response, 'Pip – I can't stand it any longer, seeing you throw yourself away on him – I'm sorry to be the one to tell you, but you *have* to know – he is married.' I stared dumbly at Pattie. 'It's not true,' I said. How could it be? 'It is,' she answered, more gently. 'My friend Marjorie works in Accounts, and she told me some time ago. He does have a wife, I didn't want to tell you, but I couldn't just keep quiet about it any longer. You can ask at Accounts yourself. They will tell you. Oh Pip, I *am* sorry.'

Cecil – married? But how could I not have known? Yet his care for me, his gentleness, his generosity – they had not been a sham, I didn't understand. Nothing added up. I wrote to him, telling him what Pattie had said, asking him if it were true, whilst at the same time begging him to say it wasn't. I still couldn't believe it yet I knew Pattie had no reason to make up a lie. And she *had* tried to warn me before. I waited for Cecil's reply. Days went by, and there was nothing. Then he arrived in person. He had travelled all night and there were dark rings round his eyes, and the lines on his face seemed deeper. Where before, I would have flung myself into his arms, I stood wordless, just staring at him.

It was all true. He was married. 'Why didn't you tell me?' I finally managed. 'I didn't want to lose you,' he said, 'and I knew I would if I told you.' He looked as stricken as I felt – and now we couldn't comfort each other. He was also right. I took off my turquoise ring which had meant so much, and offered it back. He wouldn't take it. I returned it to its box and put it away. I refused to see Cecil again after that, not even knowing when he left. I was stunned and empty. Some days later, one of the other Rhodesians, walking back to the billets, fell into step beside me and said, 'Sorry to hear you and Cecil have broken up, Pip.' 'He was married,' I said bitterly. 'Yes – but he was getting a divorce you know,' Pat informed me. But Cecil hadn't said anything about a divorce. He had said, 'If you had to know, I wish it could have been whilst I was at Sywell. I could have flown my Tiger Moth into the ground.' Perhaps neither of us was very rational. But it was too late. The shock had been too great. The dream was over. Some who heard about it wagged their heads and said, 'Oh dear, the usual story – never mind, Pip, plenty more fish in the sea!' Strangely, I found after a while, that I had no ill-feelings toward

Cecil. I believed his feelings had been genuine – or perhaps I just wanted to believe – it didn't matter which. Even stranger was the sudden realisation that the deep, and I had thought, enduring bond I had shared with him – the tenderness and the romantic love – had simply drained away. I couldn't understand it. I felt free – though I didn't want to be free – yet. How *could* it all disappear like morning mist on the airfield? Well, it had. I put it, for want of a better reason, under the heading of 'experience'.

There were new faces in Flying Control. America was now in the war, and a steady flow of servicemen from the States had been arriving over here. Whilst USAAF bases were being constructed, American Flying Control officers came to some of our airfields to gain experience of conditions in this country – vastly different from those in the USA, especially with regard to the weather.

We had four officers, including two pilots awaiting postings, Mac and Smithy. Mac was big, likeable, and an inveterate girl chaser, trying out his charm on all of us. He was great fun – but not to be taken seriously. Joan teased him, running off with his pilot's wings which she had unpinned from his jacket whilst it hung over a chair back. 'He chased me round the Control room – all night! – Well, when no one else was there!' she announced dramatically. 'And I still haven't given him his wings back!' She returned them in her own time. Mac took it all in good part. He seemed to like us all, whatever we did.

Smithy was altogether different. Tall, slimly built, blond, straight hair combed smoothly back – and rather arrogant. He seemed distant, disdainful. We were not sorry when he was posted, though when Mac left us we missed his cheerful good nature. The other two Americans were older, though Bob Donovan was probably not much over 30; I regarded him as middle-aged. 'Hank' Hankins was even older. He treated us with an old-fashioned courtesy which we loved. Bob was a quiet, efficient man with a great sense of humour. We paid him the compliment of thinking him 'just like an Englishman'. I wonder if he would have appreciated that!

An Australian FCO also arrived. He wore RAF blue, and pilot's wings. He had come over to England at his own expense to join up – if he had joined the RAAF he would still be in Australia, he said. He and Bob Donovan soon became good friends. Sometimes, as I sat at the bench in Flying Control he would give my hair a friendly ruffle in passing, and referred to me as 'Curlytop'. Our civilian recorders were all coming up to the age for retirement, and one after another, left us. Just before Mr Jones, the oldest of the three, departed, Mr Cabourne arrived to take over the watch. I was lying, half asleep, on the rest bed in our cloakroom, waiting to take my turn at logging when our aircraft started to return. The two recorders came in, one to hang up his hat and coat and the other to garb himself for the journey home. They were talking in low voices. Mr Jones said, 'Pretty little thing, isn't she? Look at those eyebrows!' 'Humph!' snorted Mr Cabourne. 'They're probably painted on!' Filled with indignation at this, I wanted to sit up and say 'Just try rubbing them off then!' Only I had kept my eyes closed until then–perhaps it would give Mr Jones too much of a shock if I erupted – and as he was just about to retire, so I let my 'painted' eyebrows pass, and lay doggo.

Soon, our three civilians were gone and Hilda, a WAAF, came to replace them during the day. We R/T operators rather resented this at first – we didn't want any more WAAF around Flying Control. But we soon took to Hilda. Her golden hair and good looks were matched by a pleasant disposition, and we felt rather mean over our initial reaction.

A Canadian FCO joined us. There was an average of four more-or-less permanent Flying Control officers plus two or three or four others who stayed briefly – perhaps weeks, perhaps months. Our Canadian stayed several months, and was adored by all of us. Flying Officer Stanley was a big man, tall and almost completely bald. He was firm and decisive, but treated us with great thoughtfulness and kindliness. There was no trace of condescension in his manner; with some FCOs we were instinctively aware that we were considered a different breed, however polite they might be towards us, but we looked forward to going on watch when Stan was there. It was a sad day when he was posted.

Pattie was posted to Manston, much to her disgust. She didn't want to leave Waddington. However, it gave a bit of leeway for room swapping, and I was now able to move into a billet with Sally and Joan. James fixed us up with an extremely unauthorised electrical appliance, Electric Joe. This was a heater to boil water or make toast on, skilfully disguised to look like an innocent biscuit tin when the lid was on. James also taught us to repair fuses, should Electric Joe cause one to blow. EJ's power supply came from the light socket, as did that of the electric irons we were not allowed to use in the billet. We were thus saved from having to report blown fuses, and the possibility of bringing to light our heinous crime – the possession of an electric heater. Using 15-amp fuse wire seemed a good idea to us.

Electric Joe was a blessing. We often missed meals through sleeping after night duty, and though we fetched each other mugs of tea and jam tarts from George's, it didn't really replace a more solid meal. Now we could heat up tins sent from home. My mother generously gave up some of her 'points', using them to send me tins of beans – a top favourite – or spaghetti in tomato sauce. Toast was made with bread and marg 'borrowed' from the cookhouse, and we had a repast fit for, well, perhaps not the Gods but it suited us, and we blessed James. Sometimes during the day, when Sally and I were both in, he would call at the billet and chat to us briefly. 'Suppose a WAAF officer comes in?' we questioned. 'I'll hide under the bed – you two can sit on it. No problem.' He grinned, removing the pipe that almost seemed to grow from his mouth. We collapsed in giggles at the thought of James' six foot plus crammed under the bed, Sally and I sitting primly, close together above, and clouds of tobacco smoke issuing and billowing all around us.

I went walking with him occasionally, along Green Lane, or through Waddington village and out into green fields divided by grey stone walls. Here, we talked, in the shelter of a wall or the lee of a hedge, and it was at these times that I learned of his involvement in the Spanish Civil War, though there were no descriptions. I admired him for his courage and his ideals; and I liked to listen to his deep, slow voice, with the slight Canadian burr, from a period of living in Canada. There had been a time just before the war when a very personal tragedy had occurred; I was surprised and grateful that he could talk to me about it.

Equally, he would joke and make me laugh – as when trying to clarify for me the technicality of electrons passing over the grid of a valve: 'Like airmen, nipping after blondes?' he said. And had loaned me his extensive gen book prior to my last trade test. If I needed advice – or someone to lean on – he was there, a tower of strength. 'Buckets of blood!' was his favourite epithet, and 'How's your mother's foot?' he would bellow, on spotting me across the road. 'I only say that to my best friends,' he informed me solemnly.

5

Conversion to Lancasters

I was aware that Tim had my welfare very much at heart. Short, stocky, good natured and generous – and deeply religious – he deserved someone who understood and identified with his beliefs. It wasn't me. I liked him as I liked anyone who cared about me, and treated him more as a brother. At least, never having had a brother, I think I did. I must have pained him often, but never with intent, yet his attitude to me didn't change. Despite my lack of religious feelings, I went to the camp church occasionally – most of us from the choir did, if only to sing. Tim, though, did a bit of lay preaching if the Padre was away. He chose the subject of sin, one Sunday evening. We, in the congregation, wondered what was coming. But it was in the context of not deliberately wronging anyone – to do so deliberately was sinful – and whilst I might not have put it in the same words, I agreed with his sentiments. When he descended from the pulpit, rather flushed, we congratulated him on his sermon. It had been thoughtfully and sincerely intended. I went to the village church too sometimes; or rather, the temporary building which served as such after the bombing and destruction of the old parish church. I liked the elderly vicar. He asked our names, and remembered them, and if he heard aircraft taking off during a service, he would offer a prayer for their safe return, which always brought a lump to my throat. He would welcome us to dances at the Village Hall too; the Fleapit, as it was unflatteringly known.

Once I had the eerie experience of dancing there with a quiet, pleasant Scottish sergeant pilot, and suddenly knowing he was 'for the chop'. I knew it with a certainty. I wondered if he had any suspicion of it himself. Sure enough, on his next op, he didn't come back. Though I scarcely knew him, it made me very sad. Perhaps it was a build up of such happenings which caused a brief, minor breakdown to affect Sally, Joan, and myself one evening at choir practice. Joan was the first to succumb, rushing out of the room in tears. Sally went out to comfort her, and brought her back shortly, a little calmer. Then tears began to trickle down Sally's face. She ran out. I went out to her, and she wept on my shoulder for a few minutes, then mopped herself up; Sally was lucky – she was one of those people who could cry without looking absolutely ghastly afterwards. Neither she nor Joan could give any reason for the weeping spell. We settled down to our rehearsal again; it was almost time to pack up. And then it was my turn. A piercing sense of sadness flooded through me, causing my voice to break and my eyes to fill. Oh, God, what was the *matter* with us all! I too made for the corridor, where I sobbed my heart out. It was Frank who came out to me. He put an arm round me and gave me a handkerchief, saying, 'It's all right, Pip – it's all right,' and continued to hold me gently until I pulled myself together. I was going on duty at midnight, and there I was, looking a bleary wreck! I sponged my face in a bathroom and put on fresh makeup, whilst Frank, bless him, waited for me and walked me over to the Watch Office, chatting cheerfully. He scrutinised me carefully to make sure I was up to it before he would let me go in, but I was myself again by then.

420 Squadron moved off to Skipton-on-Swale in Yorkshire, and 9 Squadron moved in during early August. We were busier than ever as the squadrons converted on to Lancs, with the ensuing circuits and bumps, cross-countries, air-firing, fighter-affiliation, and all the other necessary exercises. We were flying round the clock. I saw Mike, the Australian FCO, on duty often. Then, we began to meet off duty too. We had to be rather careful in our meetings since WAAF and officers were not supposed to fraternise; inevitably they did. Like others, we found ways to get around it. There were excursions into the surrounding countryside, usually by way of Green Lane; once we walked to Harmston by this pleasant route and explored the little church there. Mike was a keen photographer, and took photos in the dim interior, including one of me on my knees, looking appropriately soulful, and feeling decidedly hypocritical. He also brought his camera to Control on nights of no flying – what few there were – and Sally and Joan came too, and the Americans, Bob and Hank, and anyone else who worked in Control. We were all

portrayed on film. One evening, Sally and I wore civilian tops as a change from the eternal shirt and tie – it was fortunate that no WAAF officers visited the Watch Office! In the usual run of events, Sally tended to be less lucky in the evasion of rules over such things. She and another friend of hers, Madeline, also a wireless-op at the nearby wireless station of Branston, always liked to go to dances off camp in civilian dresses. They planned to go to one in Lincoln, and as the day had started, and remained, cold and wet, they set off after tea with summer dresses under greatcoats buttoned up to the neck. They were horrified when, on arrival in Lincoln by bus, the clouds suddenly parted, the rain ceased, and the sun shone out warmly, causing the wet roads and roofs to steam; as indeed did Sally and Madeline inside the now-stifling greatcoats.

It wasn't possible even to undo the top button, as this immediately gave away the fact that no collars and ties were beneath. They sought shelter in a Forces canteen in the High Street and found room at a table with some soldiers who, seeing them wrapped up and with flushed faces, asked with concern, if they had colds – and insisted on buying them cups of hot tea! Eventually, the time for the dance approached, and walking carefully with small steps so that the dresses did not show through the vents of the greatcoats, they arrived safely at the dance hall and flung off the offending garment with great relief. Stockings and shoes were changed, make-up repaired, hair fluffed up, and in no time they were dancing, previous discomforts completely forgotten.

But there was the return to camp to follow. Neither had booked out, so they were vulnerable on that count also. At 22.30 hrs it was still light, so there was no way of hiding the buttoned-up greatcoats on a summery evening. On the way to the bus station, they caught sight of two patrolling WAAF SPs – one of whom called, 'WAAF – have you got a pass?' Neither had, of course, and they increased their pace, pretending not to hear. The question was repeated more forcefully. Sally and Madeline forgot their dainty little steps and broke into a run. So did the SPs, scenting a quarry. In the doorway of a house opening directly on to the street stood a woman, enjoying the last of the evening's light, and watching the passers-by. She suddenly found herself bundled into her own front room, the door slammed behind her, and in the company of two panting WAAFs! Sally and Madeline, in their anxiety to escape the SPs, had taken the first available refuge. As soon as they got their breath back, they apologised profusely and explained the situation – and all three broke into hysterical laughter. Fortunately no offence was taken at the forcible invasion. The victim of it was entirely on their side and, after a while, went out to inspect the bus queues as the house was almost next door to the bus station. She reported that the SPs were still prowling around, and invited the girls to stay a little longer. Again, she reconnoitred, and this time, there was no sign of the enemy, so Sally and Madeline took their leave with many grateful thanks, caught the next bus to Waddington, and managed to get back into camp undetected.

This time, there was no charge. But I worried about Sally because she was so often 'on a charge', usually for minor things like not booking out of camp, or wearing silk stockings – the sort of misdemeanour regarded as a crime only in WAAF regulations. Eventually I took it upon myself to go to the WAAF officer – the Queen Bee – to plead her cause and point out that though she had so much on her charge-sheet, they were not serious wrongdoings, merely things she had forgotten, or not thought about. What the WAAF CO thought of this, I didn't know – she could read after all! My earnest pleading must have been rather funny, but she betrayed no sign of amusement. I had the feeling that Sally was beginning to be regarded as a bad character – which I knew she was not; far from it. I acted on impulse, and afterwards it seemed decidedly self-righteous. Sally, though, had the unconscious ability to make people feel she needed protecting – perhaps from herself!

The choir repeated its concert at the Village Hall in Waddington, and again had a success, in spite of having to retrieve a well-known organist, then with 9 Squadron, from the Horse and Jockey. He was found missing just before he was due to play the accompaniment to 'Jesu, Joy of Man's Desiring'. Luckily he was still capable. Over the next few weeks, we put on the show at

Metheringham and one or two other villages in the area. We had some strange dressing rooms – boxy little rooms in village halls, and cold, stone-paved classrooms in schools. Occasionally, these had to be shared with the boys. After initial consternation, there was nothing to do but get on with it; changes of costume had to be rapid anyway, and we soon forgot to be shy.

During one concert, when Jan and I were about to do our *Dancing in the Dark* number, Mac proceeded to sing the lyric. We looked at each other – this hadn't been rehearsed. 'He's tiddley!' whispered Jan. Mac had, uncharacteristically, had a jug or two previously, and it showed. It was so *unlike* him, but still, he seemed happy! So we danced, and Mac's slightly cracked tenor rang out through the hall, and at the end, everyone clapped and cheered and shouted. Mac, by now somewhat embarrassed, apologised to us, but we didn't mind – and obviously no one else did.

A plan evolved for the production of a pantomime for Christmas; we decided on *Aladdin*, and John and Jo got down to writing it, with suggestions welcomed from any quarter. There were topical gags involving the station and the officers – chairborne types – wingless wonders – and the like. Anything went in such a production, and traditionally, there was no comeback. When the script was completed, we thought it was hilarious, and could hardly get through a reading without hysterics – we hoped this was a good sign. But Christmas was many weeks away, and anything could happen. And did.

There had been more outings with Mike on the infrequent occasions when we could be off duty together. The Flying Control Officers had a different watch system to ours, and we had to wait for a day when the two duty rosters ran together and gave us time off. Sometimes we went into Lincoln on our bicycles, making for a small, panelled tearoom near the Cathedral, where we could usually find a secluded nook to talk. Mike talked about Australia. He said he wanted to take me back there. I couldn't believe that this was happening again, and I wasn't sure of my own feelings; after my earlier experience I wasn't in too much of a hurry to commit myself. I let the situation ride, just enjoying his company. I had the impression that I could expect to lead a very different sort of life over there, if I went, and I knew his family background was considerably more affluent than anything I had known. I was deeply attracted to him – yet I had my reservations. Well, there was no hurry. I loved it when we were on duty together; and I hoped I impressed him with my efficiency when we were landing aircraft coming back from ops, though there was no time for anything but the R/T then. 'Hello Jetty, Lighthouse O-Orange, over.' 'Hello Lighthouse O-Orange, Jetty answering, prepare to land. QFE 1003. Over.' 'Hello Jetty, Maypole B-Baker, over.' 'Hello Jetty, Lighthouse Q-Queenie, over.' 'Maypole B-Baker, airfield 1,500, over. Lighthouse Q-Queenie, airfield 2,000, over.' Meanwhile, O-Orange would have called 'Funnels', as he approached the runway, and then called to say that he was down. B-Baker was then told to pancake, and started his landing run. Q-Queenie was brought down to 1,500 feet. Fresh aircraft calling up were stacked at heights 500 feet apart above the airfield circuit, given the airfield barometric pressure to set on their altimeters, and brought down 500 feet as the lowest aircraft in the stack landed. I thought how strange it must seem if, suspended above the ground, it were possible to look over all Lincolnshire and Cambridgeshire and the other eastern counties to which the bombers returned. There would be countless spinning circles – stacks of aircraft spiralling around and down – above each base. They would descend, decrease, and a few miles away, start to increase as later aircraft returned, like whirlwinds starting up, rising, and dying away.

Joan and I asked Mike if we could go and watch take-off from the ACP's caravan one evening. Normally, spectators were not encouraged near the runway, but Mike allowed it, with cautions, and in good time we took up our positions. The black and white chequered caravan stood out against the grass, bright green in the low sunlight, at the beginning of the runway in use – 26 – usually known as the green lane, though not to be confused with Ermine Street. We knew Dick, the sergeant-pilot who was ACP that night, and the Flare Party, who were gathered around the caravan waiting until their services were needed. Their job was to attend to the runway lighting, to set up glim-lamps, goosenecks, the chance-light if required, as well as the taxiing-lights to guide landed aircraft back to dispersal. We sat in the caravan, which was in touch with Control by R/T and field telephone, and chatted to Dick whilst we waited for the action to commence. Very soon, we heard the first aircraft start to rev up, and this was echoed from dispersals all around the airfield, so that the ground seemed to shake and thrum; I could feel the throbbing deep inside me, like a fierce anticipation, frightening and thrilling at the same time.

The perimeter began to be starred here and there with the red and green eyes of wing-tip navigation lights as aircraft started to taxi out. Soon, a queue of Lancasters crawled along the track towards the runway – so much throttled-back power! Dead on time, the first Lancaster appeared at the beginning of the runway. A member of the Flare Party flashed a green on the Aldis, and the great aircraft seemed to gather itself together before rumbling past us down the avenue of lights, and lifting heavily into the darkening air. The ACP rang Control: 'A-Able airborne, sir.'

Clouds began to further dim the fading light, and it was necessary to use a white Aldis to establish the aircraft letter before giving the green. One after another, they lumbered off. By the time all had gone, it was completely dark, and we were dizzy with the noise of engines and flashing lights. The silence, as we walked back round the perimeter after saying goodnight to Dick and the Flare Party, seemed to press on our eardrums as much as the noise had done earlier. It seemed superfluous to say we hoped they'd all return, so we didn't. But of course, we both knew that was what we hoped, with every fibre of our being.

We paid another visit to the station Pigeon Farm. This was a tiny, white-washed cottage with a pigeon loft at one end, situated between hangars and offices, strangely incongruous in its rusticity. A corporal gladly showed us his charges, as they cooed contentedly in their cote, taking one down, cradled in his hand, for us to stroke. Each operating aircraft carried a box of pigeons to be released in an emergency, bearing a note of the aircraft's position. Providing, of course, the pigeon survived. It was hard to connect these peaceful-looking domestic birds with such a war-like task.

Rumours, soon proved to be fact, went around that another Group was to be formed – 8 Group. Its aircraft would be the first on target and would mark it with special flares, ready for the Main Force of bombers, and it would be something of an honour to belong to it. Other than this, we knew little. Rumours always abounded, and the most unlikely-sounding ones often proved to be true. I remembered Joe, from the Watch Office, telling me about FIDO – the initials, he said, standing for Fog Investigation Dispersal Operation (it couldn't be real! – but it was). Some of our squadron crews went off to join 8 Group – Pathfinders – and *that* was real enough. And in the meantime, we – the R/T operators – had our ACW 1 board, and all passed. I don't think any of us found it easy, but we had studied hard; the small rise in pay was welcome.

An incident occurred in the WAAF section which almost caused a mutiny. After a routine FFI examination, a notice appeared on the Waafery notice board stating that a number of airwomen were found lacking in cleanliness at the FFI; as a result, showers, supervised by a WAAF officer, would be taken once a week in the Decontamination Centre by all WAAF personnel. The majority of us were livid. We bathed every day; there was plenty of hot water at the Waafery and a bath was something to be appreciated and enjoyed, especially after coming off night duty feeling tired and unfresh. I made up my mind that there would be no supervised showers for me, come what may. And the Decontamination Centre of all places! (It was probably the only placed fitted with showers on the camp, but nevertheless!) I wasn't the only one to take this decision. We felt it to be an insult to the majority because of the lack of standards of a small minority. We were not told whether they were lousy, or just plain unwashed, but whatever the reason, we were not all like it, and there was a principle at stake.

Notices and threats appeared with increasing frequency on the notice board regarding the non-attendance at compulsory showers. I still didn't go. Eventually, a long list of names went up, including mine, with the order to report to the WAAF CO. A line of us stood, mutinous, in the corridor outside her office. A hectoring tone was adopted when my turn came – which was early as my name was near the beginning of the alphabet. But I knew what I was going to say, and proceeded to say it despite interruptions of 'Beck – be quiet!' from the WAAF Admin NCO, Sgt Norris, who was in attendance. I said, 'Ma'am, most of us here bath every day because we prefer to. It is degrading to us to insinuate that we are incapable of keeping ourselves clean. If there are those who don't care to, then they are the ones to have supervised showers, and it's known through the FFI who they are. I do not wish to attend the showers.' I knew I was sticking my neck out, and expected at least a week's CC. However, I was given only three days' jankers. I was astonished, and wondered if the CO had recognised that there was some justice in what I'd said. *Some* punishment obviously had to be meted out for disobedience. Her manner however, did not relax, and I was surprised to learn later that others had been given seven days' jankers. My 'sentence' affected me very little because of my shifts, as it happened. I scrubbed a floor in the Waafery one evening, and that was about the sum total. After a while, the shower edict quietly faded into oblivion. The WAAF officer who was responsible was posted away in the normal course of duty, and WAAF life returned to an even tenor.

I had to pay a brief visit to Sick Quarters soon after. The door of my room slammed in a gust of wind, catching my right forefinger, squashing the top and removing the nail completely. WAAF Sick Quarters dressed it and sent me over to see the MO. He was a Scot, humorous, kind, altogether a very nice man, and an excellent doctor. 'Well, lassie, you've made a fine mess of that!' he pronounced, after examining my revoltingly pulpy fingertip. He bound it up carefully and told me I was to take 48 hours off duty, and rest. I protested that I was perfectly all right, but he was adamant, so I had to go over to Control and explain to the SFCO. I always had the feeling that he didn't really approve of me, though I wasn't clear why – perhaps because of my friendship with Mike. I said I'd come on duty anyway, as two of the other girls were on leave. He refused my offer – rather coldly – and said I had better obey the MO's instructions, whilst somehow managing to convey that he didn't agree with them in spite of what he said. I left, feeling depressed and suddenly shaky, thankful after all for my time off. Back at Control after my short absence, I was the cause of much amusement as I wrote in the logbook with my forefinger in its bulky bandage pointing straight up!

The pantomime and concert rehearsals now commenced in earnest. It had been decided to stage the show in two halves – the first to be a variety of songs, dances, piano solos by Mac, some choral numbers, and a turn by a conjuror who had offered his services. The second half would be the panto, as it wasn't a lengthy production. We were sure it must be good as it still made *us* laugh. I was the Principal Boy, and Frank, my 'Princess'. I had solos, and duets to practise with Frank, as well as several dances, and plenty of stage business to learn. And my lines too, which were coming along quite well. Frank was also teaching Sally a tap-dance number, which she soon performed with verve and panache. John and Jan were busy working on Noel Coward's *The Stately Homes of England*. We thought John would never get the hang of it – he was very shy and reserved, and tended to sound wooden in spite of having the right accent; eventually he gained confidence and shed some of his reserve. Then he began to enjoy it.

Two blows fell. Mike was posted to the Middle East – and I was posted to Skellingthorpe. Mike managed to get 48 hours' leave before departing for Blackpool, where he was to embark, and I did likewise. We went home, to Buckingham. It wasn't a very happy leave, with his departure so imminent, and soon his departure could be postponed no longer. I went with him to Winslow station, and in no time the train was there... then puffing away into the grey November afternoon; I could see his arm waving until the train vanished into the distance. I stood alone on the platform and tried not to cry. Mike had repeated his proposal of marriage, when it was all over, but when would it be all over – and what sort of people would we be then?

I left for camp with my feelings in a state of confusion, and very depressed.

Consternation reigned in the Concert Party over my posting,

which I hadn't then got around to thinking about, though it was to take effect in a few days' time. I had no understudy, and it would be next to impossible for me to get over from Skellingthorpe for rehearsals, but there seemed no way out of it. I packed my kit sadly and prepared to leave. Everything was falling apart I thought drearily. John promised to see the Entertainment's Officer, and if that availed nothing, to tackle the Station Commander as he was believed to be interested in our efforts. I was too despondent to believe he'd have any success.

And so I went to Skellingthorpe. First impressions relieved my depression slightly. The half dozen or so Nissen huts of the WAAF site occupied sylvan surroundings. The trees had not quite lost their leaves and the air was fresh and sweet – and morning and evening a robin tinkled his cool, wistful song in the branches. The place seemed remote and peaceful. It didn't solve anything – but I felt better. I cycled out to the tiny Watch Office. In comparison with Waddington's spacious Flying Control this seemed almost comic. It was a small square room on the first floor, with windows all round, and a stove contained in a brick chimney in the middle. A desk occupied the space under the front windows, and on the left, a door opened to the outside staircase, also giving access to a small balcony. It was all rather cosy.

Two Flying Control Officers shared duties with a grounded sergeant-pilot, though he had lost his stripes, for what reason I didn't know. He now ranked as an AC 1. He, Bill, was usually left in charge when there was no flying, otherwise it would have been 24 hours on and 24 hours off for the two FCOs. They recognised that he was capable of dealing with an emergency should one crop up, until one of them could be contacted, though this arrangement would probably not have received official approval! I had met Bill at Waddington previously, so was not completely among strangers; the same sort of things made us laugh, and we shared many a giggle. The usual disciplines seemed more relaxed here, but a call on the R/T brought us back to normal routine instantly.

It was disrupted one afternoon, though not with intent, by one of the Met Officers from the office below. The Meteorologists still had civilian status, having not yet received RAF commissions, though this was to come quite soon. Footsteps clattered up the stairs outside, and the Control Room door burst open. The Met Man rushed in looking extremely agitated. 'That aircraft – it must come back – some bad weather is developing!' he panted. The aircraft was a 50 Squadron Lancaster which had taken off a few minutes earlier on a cross-country. The FCO had just gone over to the Mess for lunch, and Bill and I were on our own. Without giving us time to reply, the Met Man grabbed the mike from my hand – I had been about to give the aircraft a call – and attempted to call it himself. He got the call-sign right, though his procedure was non-existent. He got no reply; he tried again, but it seemed no one was listening out. By this time he was even more agitated, his hair standing on end as he ran his fingers through it, his thick-lensed glasses askew. 'Never mind,' I said soothingly. 'It can be contacted on W/T and told to return.' Bill was already on the phone to DF, asking them to pass the message, and the Met Officer subsided and returned to his own domain, muttering. The FCO returned shortly after this scene had been enacted, and we explained what had occurred.

'So he used the mike himself, did he?' said the FCO, smiling thoughtfully. The following day, the Met Officer appeared again, wearing a worried expression, to enquire if I'd logged his R/T call. 'Oh yes – all calls must be logged,' I told him. 'Oh – Oh dear!' He looked positively haggard. I then learned that the FCO on duty the previous day had set him up with an entirely fictitious story that the Group invigilating van had been in the vicinity, listening out. They had heard the Met Man's call with its lack of correct R/T procedure and had made enquiries as to the originator. The FCO had continued, 'It's a very serious offence, old boy, for an unauthorised person to use the R/T. I tried to explain to them – but you could be in for some trouble.'

The Group invigilating van was an imaginary creation – but the Meteorologist didn't know this and was too worried to think of enquiring. The unfortunate man, though said to be brilliant at his job, was very unworldly in other matters, and tended to be the butt of countless practical jokes. Life in the RAF must have been very confusing for him. He went around for days looking strained and on edge; goodness knows what the atmosphere in the Met Office must have been like – unsettled at least. Of course, nothing further happened about the incident, and the FCO told him: 'You were very lucky – probably because you're not actually in the Service yet. Watch out when you are though – you won't get off so lightly!'

I had been at Skellingthorpe for about ten days, when the news came that I was to return to Waddington! Obviously strings had been pulled, and though I was now quite at home at Skelly, I couldn't help being jubilant at the thought of getting back to Waddo and my friends and the panto rehearsals. The break, though, had helped to take my mind off Mike's departure to some extent so there had been a bonus value. I hoped for letters from him soon. I repacked my kit, said goodbye to Bill and the rest of the Watch Office staff, who had made my brief stay so pleasant, and caught the transport to Waddo.

John had been as good as his word and seen the Entertainment's Officer, who had gone to talk to the SFCO about my possible return; he met with a firm refusal. As he was a pilot officer and the SFCO a squadron leader, he couldn't argue. John next approached the Station Commander, and it was on his instructions that I had been recalled. I felt flattered that strings had been pulled in such high places on my account; I also knew I'd better be good enough to justify it. The SFCO was not unnaturally nettled over the countermanding of his decision, and was heard to mutter, 'Anyone would think this was just a bloody concert party instead of a war!' So I made absolutely sure that rehearsals encroached in no possible fashion on my duties. Not that they had done previously; perhaps he thought they might begin to as production time grew nearer, but I was determined that this would not happen.

James was going off for an interview – he had applied for a commission as an Education Officer some time earlier. Before he went, I pressed his best blue for him, fully aware of the importance of the occasion, and saw him off, wishing him luck at Waddington station. It was a fairly foregone conclusion that he would be accepted but 'it was, of course, entirely due to my smart turnout, and the wonderful creases in my trousers!' he assured me, his eyes twinkling. He was gleeful at going from AC2 to pilot officer at a stroke.

'*You* should apply for a commission,' James said. 'I see no reason why you shouldn't get one.' 'Me?' I thought incredulously. But I had lost no time in putting in an application for a posting to MEF, in the hope of at least being able to see Mike sometimes and didn't want to do anything to upset that possibility. Later Miss Shepherd, our WAAF CO, sent for me to tell me she was very sorry to say that as an only child I would not be eligible for such a posting. Air Ministry policy was that only daughters should not be sent abroad because of the extra risk to life from enemy action. So that was that, and I must be satisfied with letters and photos, which I had just begun to receive in irregular batches from Mike. A commission didn't seem very important and I thought no more about it.

The weather was becoming cooler, and one morning the camp awoke to a dense white fog. I was on duty, and as there was no possibility of flying the FCO had gone back to the Mess, leaving Jimmy, a grounded sergeant-observer, and myself in charge. About the middle of the morning we were surprised to hear the noise of aircraft engines above. Not surprising was the Darky call which came up on R/T. I answered, giving his position, but received no acknowledgement, though we could still hear his engines. I gave a second call, still with no response. Jimmy decided to go down to the pyrotechnic store and send up a rocket so that the pilot up there could at least pinpoint the airfield. He thrust a Very pistol into my hand and told me to stand on the balcony and fire it the moment I heard the aircraft come over again if he wasn't ready to send up the rocket. I had never used a Very pistol before – didn't I remember someone saying they had a kick like a mule if you weren't careful? Still, there was no help for it. If I heard the aircraft, of course I must fire it, and I held it at arm's length, finger on the trigger. I had left the R/T on the loudspeaker, but no further calls came, and I lost all sound of the aircraft's engines. Then Jimmy was back, and I dropped my arm with a sigh of relief. We heard engine sounds again in the distance, muffled by fog; I called on R/T and Jimmy sent up a couple of rockets, with a whoosh and a trail of sparks that vanished into the murk. But the engines died away completely and we heard no more. I hoped that the aircraft found its destination safely; it wasn't the sort of weather in which to get lost.

We had more Darky calls that day – some from aircraft flown by Poles, who often switched to transmit before they made their call, and it was strange to hear the incomprehensible language as they talked among themselves on the intercom. Then would come the heavily-accented ''Allo Dar-rky, 'Allo Dar-rky...' It was not always easy to understand them, but they had their own difficulties – a strange country and a strange language. It was said that they would fly in anything, no matter how bad the weather. There were calls from Americans too, and the drawling, rather toneless voices did not come over well on R/T, words seeming to run together, until we grew used to it. They used terms like Roger and Wilco – quite new to us, but which were soon adopted into our own R/T procedure.

By night, the fog had cleared, but there were no ops laid on for us, so the airfield lay quiet under the night sky. Coming off duty at midnight, I took a short cut through a hangar – and wished I hadn't. My footsteps echoed eerily in the huge, silent space, and though the hangar doors at the far end were open, the darkness was so intense as to be almost tangible, and the shape of an aircraft under whose wing I passed more felt than seen. I was glad to emerge into the comparative brightness of a starlit, though moonless night. Outside were several parked Lancasters, reminding me of enormous moth-like insects, silent, brooding, and dark against the sky. 'Waiting for their prey,' I thought. But their prey was far from here. On, past the petrol dump, across a corner of the airfield, through a gap in the hedge and out on to the main road – and then, my billet and bed.

The next afternoon on duty I began to feel rather unwell, shivery and hot by turns, with an aching head and sore throat. Hobby, the FCO, saw that I was flushed, and laid a hand on my forehead. 'You've got a temperature – off to the MO with you, my girl,' he said, and rang Sick Quarters to say he was sending me over. It was the Scots MO whom I'd seen before and liked.

'I'm afraid it's the WAAF Sick Bay for you lassie – you've got laryngitis,' was his verdict. 'I'll be in to look at you tomorrow.' I trailed miserably back to Control to tell them the news and collect my belongings. It *would* have to happen just now when we were short-handed anyway – and what would the SFCO say? He would think me more of a nuisance than ever, I was convinced. And the concert date was rapidly approaching – I would be missing important rehearsals – I was nearly in tears.

The MO had phoned Hobby to tell him I was to go off duty immediately and he said when I appeared woebegone, 'Never mind, m'dear, you go to Sick Bay and get well soon.' I wonder what he would have thought if at that moment I had done what I felt like doing – laying my head on his RFC wings and having a good cry! Dear, kindly Hobby – he probably wouldn't have minded. Over at WAAF Sick Quarters I was soon lying quietly in a cool bed letting my anxieties slip away. I'd cope with them when I was better. Sally and Joan came to see me in the first few days; I could hardly speak – my voice was no more than a hoarse whisper. Later, during the rest of the two weeks I spent in Sick Bay, all the gang visited me at different times: Sally and Joan again, Tim, John, Frank and Mac – all most concerned, and imploring me to get well soon.

At last I was out and about again – back on duty, and, working at concert rehearsals. Jo and I were going to prepare the playbills. A title had to be decided on for our production – 'Concert and Pantomime' seemed bald and unimaginative; discussion ranged over alternatives, none of which seemed sufficiently descriptive. John suggested 'Divertissement'. This pleased most of us but 'supposing people don't know what it means' queried someone. We decided to risk that, and John's proposal was adopted. Our posters featured a scantily-dressed girl, as well as a list of attractions, which we hoped would make everything clear, and Jo and I worked on enough to display at strategic points around the camp. Finally, it was time for the panto dress rehearsal. The concert items had already had their final run through and we were happy with them. My main worry was again the non-arrival of a parcel containing the evening dress I was to wear in the choir numbers – particularly the gold high-heeled sandals I needed to wear as Aladdin so that I'd be at least as tall as Frank, my princess. It would be absolute disaster if they didn't arrive.

Frank and I practised our dances to the tunes of *Lucky Me, Lucky You* and *Back to Back*, and we sang *You've Done Something to my Heart* to each other, soulfully. I trilled *Only You,* and *Dearly Beloved*, though Jan still insisted *I'm Old-Fashioned* would have been a better contrast. *Moonlight Becomes You* was another of my solos. *Me and my Girl* provided our opening number, and two more choruses came from the Disney film, *Bambi – Love is a Song* and *April Showers*. Poor Tim was stuck with another Disney offering, *Der Fuehrer's Face*, which featured distressing 'raspberry' noises.

Like most dress rehearsals, this one was lengthy and fumbling; lines were fluffed, a dance routine went wrong. It was all *awful*. We came away at last, thoroughly depressed. Of course, there were the inevitable attempts to cheer ourselves up with 'It'll-be-alright-on-the-night' remarks. We hoped it would be. The missing parcel turned up. And the night arrived. Peeping through the stage curtains in the NAAFI, we watched the rows of chairs gradually being occupied. There were an awful lot of chairs. The first few rows were reserved for officers – and the Station Commander was sitting in the middle of the front row. Our 'Divertissement' commenced, and individual acts and choral numbers reeled off quite successfully. At least, we hoped they were. I stood in the wings with Sally listening to Mac's sparkling performance of Chopin's *Valse Brillante*, which we particularly loved, and so strung up were we that we could hardly restrain ourselves from rushing on to the stage and dancing to the lilting music. Sally fiercely chewed her handkerchief instead.

A problem emerged. It was all going on for longer than we'd anticipated – no one had thought to time the acts! Still, we were almost at the end of the first half. Our final turn was the conjuror, whose act we hadn't seen previously; he had assured us he was a professional. If so, he must have had an off night. Trick after trick went wrong, and he persisted in starting others in an effort to get one at least to work, ignoring hissed requests from the wings to get off the stage. The audience was in an uproar – boos and jeers and ironic laughter came from the erks – it seemed like total disaster. *Why* hadn't we asked him to go through his act at rehearsal? *Why* hadn't someone timed the first half? Some people were leaving the hall. The curtain was rung down hastily on him and he was dragged from the stage, still protesting angrily.

The Station Commander stood up and turned round. 'Quiet!' he ordered, in a voice which carried through the hall. 'Give them a chance!' The audience subsided, to our inexpressible relief. We announced a fifteen-minute interval for refreshments, and rushed to change into our costumes and make-up for the pantomime. Most of my Aladdin costume had been supplied by Joan; black satin briefest-of-brief shorts, and a filmy blouse patterned in narrow stripes of brilliant colour, with full sleeves and buttoned cuffs. I had a coolie hat which I'd made, and leg make-up, as stockings were not available. I just hoped the patch of Elastoplast on my knee wouldn't be too obvious. I had fallen off my bike taking a corner too sharply a few days previously, cutting and grazing my knee rather badly – and wondering what else could happen. I hadn't imagined our conjuror then.

The entire cast seemed to be milling about and talking at once. I felt dreadful – more like crying than portraying the bright, glowing personality who would presently run out on to the stage. No, I couldn't do it, I'd be hopeless – my fingers trembled so much that I was unable to fasten the buttons on my cuffs. Then Frank arrived at my side – Frank, dressed in his sister's blue evening gown and wearing a golden wig, made up to look like a girl and looking very much in drag. He took my wrist and quickly fastened the buttons I couldn't cope with, then squeezed my hand with both of his. 'Good luck, Pip,' he said smiling, 'You'll be alright!' The warm affection in his voice comforted me, and suddenly I knew I *would* be alright, and blessed Frank for his understanding and thoughtfulness. The curtain went up for the opening chorus, and as the last strains of 'For Me and my Girl' died away, I leapt out on to the stage crying an immortal opening line, 'Hello, boys!' I was greeted with an appreciative chorus of wolf whistles and clapping, which did wonders for my morale.

From then on everything went perfectly. The comedy was fast and furious; Tim as Widow Twankey, and Jo as Uncle

Abenazer, were a riot. Tim's ample padding of a couple of large balls of wool and cushions strapped fore and aft, went a little awry, as one ball of wool sagged lower than the other and his rear cushion drooped, giving a distinctly odd appearance. He was well able to exploit this, and the audience rocked. Sally did her tap number, and was loudly applauded. I sang my solos and duets with Frank, and we danced. It was great, exuberant fun, and Frank, being the professional he was, made everything easy for me. The climax was a glorious mix-up, with characters chasing each other round the stage and ending up in a heap in the middle – then leaping up for the final chorus. The clapping was loud and enthusiastic, and we knew it had gone well. Frank and I took bows alone – and how sweet *that* applause was! It made up for all the nervous anxieties suffered earlier.

When the curtain finally came down and the hall emptied, we had a back-stage party at which I could stay only briefly, as I was on duty at midnight. Expecting that I'd feel rather drained, I had taken the precaution of obtaining some caffeine tablets from Sick Quarters as I knew there were ops that night, and I needed to stay alert.

The kites were due back soon after midnight and shortly before the first ETA, the Station Commander, as was his custom, came in, accompanied by the MO. Seeing me at the bench, he came over and congratulated me on my performance, saying that he had enjoyed it immensely. The MO followed this by exclaiming 'Ye were fine lassie-just fine!' I glowed with pleasure at this praise. Then came the first call on R/T, and for the next hour or so, all thoughts of the concert were banished from my mind.

Christmas 1942 was almost upon us. I was not having Christmas leave, but there were dances and festivities on the camp to look forward to, and I had to admit that whilst going home was a nice thought, it would have been very quiet, and after the first couple of days, rather boring. That might have been preferable to the very unpleasant incident which marred the celebrations for me and proved to be rather more than just an incident for the other people involved. About a week before Christmas, I came off duty at midnight and had settled down thankfully to sleep, having said goodnight to Ina, who also shared the room. Joan was on duty, so no one else would be in that night. Ina appeared absorbed in a book, which she was reading by the light of a torch. Already half-dreaming, I was jerked back to wakefulness by the door opening softly, and then someone half-sprawling over my bed, which was nearest the door. 'Who's that?' I demanded, sitting up with some rapidity. But Ina's voice whispered across from the other side of the room, 'Over here, Lennie!' Then I recognised the intruder as a New Zealander Ina went around with. 'Oh, Lennie – for goodness' sake get out!' I said anxiously. But Lennie took no notice, and Ina's torch was extinguished now, though I could hear their low voices.

The rules were that in such a situation one should call the NCO in charge of the house – but I didn't want to do that, and neither did I wish to know what was to follow. In fact I didn't know what to do – it was a situation I didn't have the experience to cope with. I lay down and pulled the bedclothes over my head, feeling sick and embarrassed, longing to be anywhere but there. The sound of shoes and jacket dropping to the floor made me stop my ears, and I hardly dared move. I think I must have willed myself to sleep, as I had no recollection of anything after that. I would have preferred to forget the whole thing – but unfortunately some of the girls in the room below had heard Lennie's voice and other tell-tale sounds, and next morning asked me what had been going on. I told them briefly, and said I didn't want it to go any further. The more I thought about it the more distasteful it became and I wanted to erase it from my memory. Two of the girls were not prepared to let it rest. Ina was not liked very much; her affairs were, inevitably, the talk of the Waafery. Philippa, from downstairs, announced that if I would not report the incident to the WAAF CO, she would. Judy supported her. When Joan heard about it, she agreed.

This left me in the difficult position of having to do it myself, or leaving it to Philippa, who left me in no doubt that she would do so, and thus being in trouble myself for not reporting it. Whether rightly or wrongly, I decided I'd better do it myself, though I had no taste for it. I knew that Miss Shepherd would at least be understanding. She listened sympathetically whilst I explained what had occurred, and pleaded that this should be the end of it. Of course, this was too much to hope for. She completely understood my feelings, she said, but it was a serious breach of discipline, and since an airman was involved, it would have to be reported to the Station Commander. A charge would be brought against them both, and I would be the witness. Seeing the shock on my face she continued, 'I am sorry – but you have done the right thing.'

I dreaded the hearing, and the outcome. What had happened was their business and, apart from protesting to Ina, I would have let it pass. Now it was all to come out, and they would be punished and it was my fault; I longed for someone to advise me, but there was no one. Eventually we were marched before the Station Commander, and I had to repeat my evidence in front of the two concerned; a very different role to that in which I'd last been seen by the Group Captain. I felt sick and ashamed – the more so when I later learned that Lennie's punishment of detention in the glasshouse, harsh as that was, would prevent him becoming aircrew, for which he'd been accepted. I knew he would never forgive me for that. Ina was confined to camp for two weeks, and lost two weeks' pay. I felt wretched about the whole business.

But Christmas was still to come. I went to a tea-dance at the Waafery on Christmas Eve, alone. I didn't have much heart for it. Sally was on a course at Compton Bassett and I missed her company badly. The evening, when I was on duty, was enlivened by a number of telephone calls, mostly from the Officers' Mess with all sorts of crazy requests – the callers being in various stages of intoxication! Later still, the CO of 1661 Conversion Unit arrived, insisting that he was in control of operations – it was vitally necessary to co-operate with neighbouring stations in the emergency recovery of Father Christmas, who was in serious trouble; three of his four reindeers' antlers had been feathered! This called for very careful judgment, and was I believe, successful. But then, S/Ldr Murray was a very experienced pilot, with a tour on 207 as a Flight Commander to his credit – and anyone who could survive a tour on Manchesters could *fly*, and was also lucky! I thought him handsome and rather dashing. Well – Father Christmas was in luck *that* night!

Back in November the King had visited Waddington – an event I missed, partly because I had come off a hectic night duty that morning and was too tired to stay up, and partly because I was so indignant that, in preparation for the visit and the ensuing bulling-up, many gallons of aircraft fuel had been used to clean the hangar floors. When I thought of the risks constantly endured by the Merchant Navy to get the fuel to this country, I couldn't forgive what seemed like a wanton waste. Not that I was blaming the King for this! And since no one knew about my protest, it was pretty futile anyway.

Apparently expressing disapproval of all parades, one of 9 Squadron's pilots, Andy Storey, turned up for a parade rehearsal for the Royal visit wearing carpet slippers, claiming Stores had no shoes to fit his long feet! Not only this, but he brought along a very small dog on a very long lead to further confound matters. This story went the rounds of the camp. I didn't hear of the consequences, if any, of this piece of clowning, but it caused much hilarity and approval, except among the disciplinarians. The Station Warrant Officer was reported to have been on the verge of apoplexy.

I had seen Andy around the camp – one could hardly miss him since he was about 6ft 4in tall and towered above his crew like a mountain above foothills. I remembered him watching take-off one evening from the Watch Office balcony, and as his Flight Commander and friend S/Ldr Jarret was clearing the runway in Z-Zola, he lifted an arm high, crossing his fingers. He didn't lower it till the Lancaster was out of sight. Apart from this, I did not actually meet Andy until New Year 1943, when I went to a dance at the NAAFI. He must have remembered me from Flying Control and came over to ask me to dance a Viennese waltz with him. With the great difference in our heights I wondered how we'd manage – but he swept me around with assurance and ease and, certainly on my part, with great exhilaration for I loved waltzing. If the music was by Strauss, I danced in a dream of flying skirts and gallant partners and Andy *was* a gallant partner, with grace and panache.

Afterwards, we sat and regained our breath and talked. I was astonished to learn that his home was in Boston, USA, for he spoke without any trace of an American accent. There was nothing about this tall man with the high forehead and pale, sensitive face and the fair, sweeping, typically RAF moustache which suggested America. Andy sat with one leg loosely resting across his other knee, and as we talked, one of his crew came along, paused to exchange a greeting, then swiftly bent and seized Andy's uppermost foot and gave it a sharp twist. 'Oh, you bloody fool!' he groaned, as the gunner moved rapidly off, grinning wickedly. Turning to me Andy explained, 'Although I'm big, I'm not very well put together, and a jerk like that on any of my joints puts them out of action for hours – as he -', nodding after the disappearing gunner, 'well knows! I won't be able to dance again tonight – but I can get a drink; will you stay and talk to me?' He limped painfully over to the bar, returning with drinks, and I marvelled at his unruffled acceptance, and even amusement, at his gunner's mischievous, and to my mind, unkind, act. No doubt Andy had his own methods of revenge! He told me of his home in Boston, his college years at Harvard, and how he then came to join the RCAF: 'I felt America should be taking part in the war – that it was essential – but at that time we were still neutral, so the only course for me was to cross the border and join up.'

Not long afterwards the USA had entered the war, but Andy had preferred to stay in the RCAF rather than transfer to the USAAF. I was moved by the depths of his feelings for this country. 'I suppose I had everything I wanted at home,' he continued thoughtfully, 'a devoted family, lovely home, no money problems, but I had spent a long vacation in England just pre-war, and I fell in love with the country. When the war started and I heard what was happening over here – the bombing and destruction – I couldn't bear the thought of it. I couldn't sit back and close my eyes to it.' He stopped and smiled apologetically, 'Sorry to carry on like this – God! You must think me an awful bore!' and he limped off to the bar again to replenish our glasses. I had just seen a very different side to the man with the long shambling stride and the often-scruffy appearance who loved to clown. When the dance ended, he insisted on seeing me back to my billet in spite of his still-troublesome ankle, and he whistled scraps of his favourite tunes as we walked. He loved classical music, he said, but enjoyed light music as well, as the bright notes of the clever little parody, 'Bach Goes to Town', bore witness, as he whistled it expertly. The notes still ran through my brain as I got into bed. Andy had dropped a chaste kiss on my forehead, stroked my hair, and turned quickly back to the road. After that, we met around the camp sometimes, stopping to exchange news, but nothing more. I was glad since his presence raised issues in my mind concerning Mike. But Andy seemed to have unexplained reservations of his own.

His tour was almost complete. I asked him one day if he would take me up in his Lancaster – I still longed for the chance of a flight. 'When my tour's finished – it could be any time now – I promise I'll take you up for a flip.' So I had that to look forward to. In the meantime, I had a 48 due, and went home. When I got back, Andy would almost certainly have done his last op. The catchy 'Bach Goes to Town' was often in my mind, and I would find myself humming it. I started the journey back cheerfully enough, but a sense of unease crept into my thoughts which I couldn't at first account for. Then I thought, 'Andy!' But I wouldn't dwell on this possibility – I was probably worrying about nothing anyway. After all, wasn't the last op of a tour one of the easier targets? I felt sure I'd heard that somewhere. I firmly shut the burgeoning anxieties from my mind – but when I got back to Waddo, I made immediate enquiries. My forebodings had been well-founded. Andy's last trip had not been an 'easy' target. It had been Berlin. And he hadn't returned. Not again, oh, not again. I wept silent tears for this American who had loved England so much. It was New Year when I first talked to Andy. Now it was January 19th. It all seemed so crazy.

Departures were in the air. Some had already taken place. BAT Flight had moved to Fulbeck before the concert and panto, depriving us of some of the members of the choir, but Shorty, Don and George turned up for the occasion, and we were delighted to see them. I had written to James, telling him all about our efforts. He was far away in the wilds of Wigtownshire, at an Air-Sea Rescue base. There were, he wrote, two snags to the place: '1. It's too ruddy far from home; 2.

There are no aircraft here, so I can't nip off smartly for a day. Otherwise I'd have been over to Waddo ages ago! But I get out to sea on every possible occasion – it's grand fun and we get some wonderful views on good days. Apart from that, it's much more of a thrill than flying, for there's bags of breeze and salt spray and waves chucking one about the place. In rough weather when the boat is being kicked all over the seas she hits each big wave with a crash that makes your teeth rattle.'

Apropos our unfortunate conjuror at the concert, James went on to describe the fate of a conjuror at an ENSA concert he'd attended previously. He had asked for someone from the audience to help him with some card tricks, 'and the bloke who volunteered – a sergeant known to one and all as Tizer – who happened to be a conjuror also, in civil life – played merry hell with him, and made all his tricks go wrong. It was most amusing – though I felt a bit sorry for the poor old lad. I've never seen anyone look so shocked as he appeared when the card was never the right one; when Tizer produced the missing card from the other conjuror's trouser pocket, he brought the house down!' Playing to a Service audience was obviously no sinecure as far as conjurors were concerned.

Early in April, Frank was the next one to leave. He and five other SHQ Signals wireless ops were posted to the Middle East. Sally, working with them, knew them all. Her particular friend was Pete, and he, Sally, Frank and I had several light-hearted and frequently hilarious outings together. The four of us had gone into Lincoln to see the film, *For Me and My Girl*, and walked all the way back to camp in a howling gale, singing choruses from the film. When we reached Waddington village, we called on the baker, who even at that hour was busy baking jam tarts which smelled deliciously warm and sweet. We begged to buy some, and at first he refused, saying he wouldn't have enough for the next day, but at our combined pleading he relented: we went off happily consuming hot jam tarts from a paper bag in the windy dark, as we walked the remaining distance to camp. Small pleasures and a lot of laughter were the hallmarks of the relationship we all shared. It was *fun*. We needed it.

Another trip to Lincoln and the cinema, this time to see *Tales from the Vienna Woods* – my beloved Strauss waltzes! We had time for a meal before the film started, so had tea in the cinema restaurant. The tables were glass-topped, and each time I applied the pressure of my knife or fork to my plate, it started to spin on the glass beneath. This, of course, started us off, and we could hardly eat for giggles. Soon, all our plates were doing a revolution or two. 'We'll be taking off soon!' spluttered Peter. Finally, we all mopped our eyes and calmed down sufficiently to finish the meal, though a hysterical giggle bubbled up now and again. The film quietened us and we enjoyed it tremendously; at its conclusion we emerged again to sing our way back and, once out of Lincoln's environs, waltz along the path if we felt like it. In the moonlight, our high spirits were released and tensions swept away in the mood of gaiety that possessed us.

Now the time had come to say goodbye to all this. Frank, Pete, and the other W/Ops were due to leave for Blackpool, where they would embark for the Middle East. Sally and I had arranged to go and see them off at Lincoln's Central Station. She was so distressed at the thought of saying goodbye to her Peter that I was worried about her, and as she was on duty the night before, I offered to go and sit with her as I wasn't on duty myself. We talked softly through the night when she was not operating; the other W/Ops were newcomers, replacing those who were posted, so it would have been a lonely night and an inexpressibly dreary one otherwise. Morning came, and we had just time for a quick wash to remove the night's staleness and then swallow some breakfast before dashing to the guardroom, where we were to meet the boys and board the transport into Lincoln.

Frank and Pete arrived together, beaming to see us there, Frank carrying his precious fishing rods as well as a bulging kitbag. The other four arrived, and the transport only a few minutes after; only a small utility – we wondered how we'd all fit in. Kitbags were piled in two deep and we piled in on top – eight of us. Somehow we sprawled over the kitbags, arms and legs all over the place. Sally and Pete held hands tightly and Frank's arm lay over my shoulders, steadying me as the van jolted along the road. We were very happy and shrieked with laughter when Ernie's hand kept poking Len under the chin, emerging apparently disembodied from under the kitbags. Everything was impossibly hilarious.

I had a typical, light-hearted letter from Frank a few days later from Blackpool: 'The six of us were quite lucky in being able to stick together,' he wrote. 'Little Len, two of the others and myself occupy one room in the house, and Pete and his pal are in another. Len and I have been told that we should have the room for two because we keep the others awake all night with our giggling – you know me!'

9 Squadron left for the new satellite station of Bardney, and only 44 was left. We heard that Waddington would be closing down in the near future for the installation of concrete runways, as grass runways were too dangerous for the heavy Lancasters – especially bombed-up Lancs. S/Ldr Burnett was promoted to Wing Commander and became 9 Squadron's CO; Wing Commander Nettleton, the Augsburg VC, now commanded 44.

Some weeks earlier, Mac had introduced Sally and myself to two of his radar mechanics – both Canadians; Hank and Freddy. We ran into them again in Lincoln when the Easter Fair was in full swing, and they suggested we joined them as they were on their way to it. This seemed a delightful idea to us as we both adored fairs, but had little money to spend. Hank and Freddy assured us they were flush, and not to worry about it – they wanted to try all the rides in the fair!

So we started out sedately on the roundabout with splendid painted horses, eyes wide and nostrils flaring, and shining brass barley-sugar poles and steam organ – it seemed like the heart of the fair. Next, the dodgems, , the swingboats and the caterpillar – we did indeed try everything, Sally and I ending up in a mood of champagne-like exhilaration. The two Canadians we noted with surprise looked a little green round the gills.

I went with Tim to a party at the Horse and Jockey. The pilot of the aircraft Tim worked on had invited his aircrew and groundcrew, and any girl-friends they might care to bring, to join him for drinks and a meal. I knew the pilot by name and sight only; this was Cliff Shnier, a Canadian Flight Sergeant. Tim and all the groundcrew were devoted to him. A man of above-average height, lean and broad-shouldered, with very dark wavy hair and a narrow moustache below a beak of a nose: a memorable face. He walked with the grace of a big cat, and when I had seen him in the Watch Office, was aware of an aura of controlled ferocity about him. I was a little in awe of him. I'd heard it said that he was Jewish, and lived only to bomb Germany; whatever the truth, his dedication was evident.

But in the cheerful surroundings of the H & J dining room, his guests around him and drinks flowing, he was completely relaxed. Roast chicken – an H & J 'special' – was served, and Cliff got the wishbone; to my surprise, he leaned across the table to me and asked me to share the wish. We each hooked a little finger round the bone and pulled; I got the longest piece – and the wish. Cliff sat back, laughing. Silently I made my wish – someone, long ago, had once said to me, 'Always wish for happiness – your wish is sure to come true sooner or later.' So that was what I did. And I kept my piece of the wishbone for luck. Later, I wondered if things might have gone differently for Cliff if *he* had had the wish, or if I had made a wish for him instead of myself. Oh, but this was superstitious nonsense anyway… or was it?

Tim was rather pleased that Cliff had picked on his girl: 'Naturally he chose the prettiest girl at the table,' he laughed, when afterwards I expressed surprise. I enjoyed the compliment, but like all such compliments, could never quite take it seriously.

Later I asked Cliff a very special favour and decided to be daring, or perhaps cheeky. 'It doesn't matter if you say "No", though. ' 'Why, what is it?' he enquired, smiling. 'Well – would – could you take me up in your Lanc some time – on an NFT or something? I've always wanted to go up in one – but I'll understand if you can't,' I gabbled.

But he said, 'Oh, sure! I'll take you up – no problem,' and didn't seem to mind at all. 'You really *will*?' I almost danced for joy. 'Listen,' he continued, 'we're doing a low-level formation exercise tomorrow morning – be outside No. 4 hangar at 11 o'clock and I'll taxi round and pick you up there with the rest of the crew. Keep it under your hat though – it's strictly unofficial.' This I well knew. We were back on four watches and I was doing 16.30 to midnight and would be off all the following day – it couldn't have worked out better. I cycled out to the hangar at the appointed time and waited with the others of his crew, who were expecting me, whilst Cliff taxied the Lanc round from dispersal. Somehow he had scrounged a helmet and parachute for me. 'Put the helmet on,' he instructed, 'just to be on the safe side – then the bods in the other kites won't spot your curls.'

The crew made a screen around me as we walked across, and I climbed into the Lancaster. It was more than unofficial – it was completely forbidden for WAAF to fly in operational aircraft. Once inside, and the crew settled in their positions, I felt the fuselage begin to throb and tremble as the four great Merlins revved up. A surge of power swept through the Lanc as Cliff taxied her out on to the perimeter, and my suppressed nervous excitement caused me to shake almost uncontrollably. I glanced at the navigator, by whose position I'd been advised to stand, hoping he hadn't noticed my shivers. He gave me an encouraging smile. We reached the runway, paused, and thundered down it, and were airborne, my ears slowly adjusting to the noise of the engines. I was aloft in a Lanc at last.

Circling, we waited for the other two kites to become airborne. They formatted on either side of Cliff's machine, wing-tip to wing-tip – a sight more impressive than anything I could have ever imagined. The enormous wing spans stretched away on either side, each wing bearing its two great Merlins, and the three Lancs flew in line – abreast with seemingly only inches between wing tips. The skill of all three pilots was very evident, especially as we were sweeping along at what I judged to be about 150 feet! The thrill and sensation of flight was the most exhilarating feeling I thought I'd ever known. We set course for the Wash, and were speeding over flat fields and fens, watching cattle draw together, then scatter in alarm, whilst a farm worker threw himself down in terror as these monsters hurtled above him, not knowing if they were friend or foe. Then out over the Wash and the North Sea, leaden-grey and heaving sluggishly. I remembered it was the first time I'd glimpsed the sea since 1938, though then it had been at ground-level – or rather, sea-level.

A few minutes later we swept round and were flying inland again, still in tight formation. I became aware of an uncomfortable, hot sensation creeping up the back of my neck; my palms felt clammy – and my stomach heaved. Oh no! I couldn't be airsick – not now. I fought it off for as long as possible, but I couldn't win. The navigator, by whose position I was still standing, or rather, sagging, was sympathetic, and gave me his handkerchief. I felt wretchedly embarrassed at the unpleasant sight I must be presenting him with. When we landed, I miserably apologised, but Cliff and all the crew insisted that I shouldn't worry – it could and did happen to anyone at any time. They couldn't have been nicer – but I still felt it was a rotten repayment to Cliff for the risk he'd taken in letting me go along against all the rules. I cycled drearily back to the billet and went to bed for a couple of hours, until I felt ready to face the world again. Still, nothing – nothing at all – could cancel out that fabulous experience!

I saw Cliff's navigator again when I returned his boiled, washed, and ironed handkerchief. Somewhat to my surprise, he invited me out to dinner, suggesting the Railway Hotel by St Mark's Station. I would have thought he had seen more than enough of me. We arrived at the hotel and after a drink, went into the dining room. All through the soup course I chattered happily, and as the next course came, wondered why he kept giving me odd, sidelong glances. Eventually he could stand it no longer: 'Er – you have some soup on the end of your nose!' he announced, with some distaste. I blushed scarlet, and quickly removed the spot of soup with my napkin, but the evening was ruined. After this, there was clearly no chance of continuing the acquaintanceship. Soup on my nose really was *the end*!

6

Farewell to Waddington

Waddington's temporary closure drew near. The choir held a farewell party at the Horse & Jockey just before the groundcrews were due to leave. We knew this was the end of a happy era for all of us and were sad at heart, yet the evening was full of laughter, and our farewells, when they came, were merry and sentimental by turn.

Finally, 44 Squadron's aircraft departed, and we watched disconsolately from Control as they winged away one by one, to Dunholme Lodge. The last two were airborne – but something was happening: they circled the airfield, then, on an obviously prearranged plan, formatted, and flew directly at the Watch Office at 'naught' feet, only climbing away at the very last moment, one to port, the other almost vertically. We had watched, mesmerised, and a gasp of breath came from all the observers of this final, brilliant display. It was a magnificent beat-up and a great flourish of farewell. And the two pilots responsible were F/Lt Pilgrim – and Cliff Shnier. Some weeks later, news found its way back that Cliff had been commissioned and transferred to 97 Squadron, Pathfinders, at Bourn. He went missing on a Hamburg raid at the end of July. I hadn't believed it could happen to him – not Cliff, with his superb skill, confidence, and daring.

Great mounds of earth were being thrown up all over the airfield, as if giant moles were at work. Tractors, lorries and concrete mixers chugged around, and it was incredibly boring in Flying Control. Nothing on the R/T but an occasional ground-test call. I hated it. When a request came through from Bardney for two R/T operators, I jumped at it, as did Joan. The recently-promoted S/Ldr Shobbrook (who had once been an LAC Flying Control assistant – was it only last year?) was also departing for Bardney to become SFCO there. He gave Joan and me a lift in his Utility, together with our kit, for which we were grateful. As we bumped over the 'drome and out on to the flat roads of Lincolnshire, I felt light-hearted and eager to be back at work; there would be aircraft again, and flying.

I liked Bardney immediately; like Skellingthorpe it was widely dispersed but I had my cycle. Sally probably missed the use of it though! We were quartered in a Nissen hut; the accommodation was fairly primitive as the airfield had only been constructed in late '42–'43, and 9 Squadron had moved in during April. The girls with whom we shared the hut turned out to be a pleasant and thoughtful crowd. We had our beds at the end of the hut with the Met girls and Grace, the only other WAAF R/T operator, though she had trained as a radar mechanic, which secretly impressed me. She hadn't been employed as such, probably because the section was geared to men only. We had few amenities – the only built-in one was a shelf running the length of the hut on either side, which held mostly books or photos. We 'lived' out of our suitcases and bomb-boxes, as well as our kitbag. Bomb-boxes were sturdy wooden containers with rope handles at each end; I don't think it crossed our minds that the previous contents had been dropped on Germany – we were just grateful for the extra storage space.

Ablutions were at the end of the hut. The bath block was a separate, draughty building, with duckboards on the concrete floor to step onto from the bath. It was necessary to towel dry as quickly as possible and to fling clothes on; wind whistled through the ill-fitting windows and under and over the doors and chilled the bather in no time. Sometimes there was hot water, sometimes not. It wasn't unknown for those of us who wanted a bath at such times to settle for a strip-wash, using our issue pint mug full of hot water, boiled up on an illegal kettle! We had all learned long ago to carry our own bath plugs, since there never seemed to be any. Who collected them all?

Our greatest advantage was a portable gramophone belonging to Pat, one of the Met assistants. She had a good selection of records, of which the most popular, by general consent, was Bing Crosby singing *Beautiful Dreamer*, followed by Gigli's rendition of *M'appari*. *Jeannie with the Light Brown*

Hair was another favourite from Pat's collection. Occupants of Hut 6 were always recognisable by the songs they sang.

The Control Office, though larger than Skellingthorpe's brick box, was not as large as Waddington's imposing Control, though the interior layout more nearly approached it. It, like the rest of the station, had a happy and relaxed feel, and there was less formality between officers and other ranks. There were three Flying Control officers: S/Ldr Shobbrook; F/Lt Sugdon, and F/O Jack Wardle. F/Lt Sugdon was a tall, dark Canadian who had been acting SFCO. He was full of vitality and nervous energy and his face had the appearance of having been rapidly sketched-in: a gash of a mouth and straight brows set at an angle across his forehead, shooting up and down as he talked. His black hair stood on end at the slightest encouragement, with almost always a lock falling across his brow. F/O Jack Wardle was slightly below medium height, with smooth dark hair and horn-rimmed glasses. He was a soft-voiced, quiet man who was calm and efficient.

There were two men R/T operators – Ron and Syd – but they did not stay long; Ron was posted off on a course, and Syd had applied and been accepted for a Flying Control officer's course. Later, he rejoined us at Bardney, having been newly commissioned. It was difficult remembering not to call him Syd still – thought I don't think he minded. He was good-natured and easy going. Joan and I were soon at home in Control and began to know some of the pilots, it being something of a rendezvous for them when nothing was on – a good place for a cup of tea! Geoff Stout was one of the first pilots I spoke to, commenting that his name was not very apposite, since he was tall, dark, and slender. 'That,' he said, 'was not very original!' But his smile took away any sting from the remark. It had probably been said to him many, many times.

Geoff later transferred to 617 Squadron. Like Cliff, he went missing. Among the other pilots were Jack Anstee; Charles Newton – who was a lawyer in civilian life and retained something of the dry, precise manner of his profession, yet was very likeable; 'Mac' MacCubbin, who gained a DFC and completed a tour; P/O Jim Lyon, with his Lancaster christened 'Spirit of Russia'; and Sgt Livingstone. Both P/O Jim Lyon and

Sgt Livingstone completed tours and were awarded 'gongs'. Could aircrew prospects be improving? Just a little, perhaps, I hoped. Later I came to know the crew of another 'Mac' – MacHead, a devil-may-care New Zealander. On a day off I had gone to Lincoln alone, as was usually the case since when I was off duty, Joan was on. I had caught the early evening bus back. Gazing idly out of the window, I watched a Halifax flying at about 1,500 feet, as near as I could judge, travelling in the same direction as the bus, though some miles away to the south. As I watched, the aircraft seemed to falter – and then just fell out of the sky. We all saw the explosion as it hit the ground; there was a moment of silent horror before exclamations and questions broke out. The driver carried on. There was nothing we could do – help would have been sent by observers closer than we were. I never knew where it came from or heard any more about it. Just an incident glimpsed from a bus window, but an incident which meant the deaths of seven men. It was so shockingly casual.

Perhaps it was this experience which caused me not to snub the little Canadian W/Op AG who attached himself to me as I walked the quarter mile from the main camp to the WAAF guardroom. He was a little tight – just a trifle unsteady on his feet – but very apologetic about it. He had seen the crash too. 'Poor devils,' he muttered. Then, brightening, 'Say! I haven't seen you around before -where do you work?' I told him. 'Gee! I must look you up!' I thought I'd better warn him that visits and phone calls were strictly against regulations at Flying Control. Opposite the entrance to WAAF Quarters, an empty tar barrel stood up-ended by the roadside. The Canadian sat on it. 'Excuse me,' he begged. 'I want to talk to you but I can't stand up any more – forgive me if I sit here.' He tried to make a date with me; I gently but firmly put him off, and said I must go. Reluctantly he rose, or rather tried to rise, from his tar-barrel seat; he hadn't seen the patch of still-tacky tar on it – which was now adhering to the seat of his pants. 'Aw hell!' he moaned. I wanted desperately to giggle, but managed to suppress the desire, with some difficulty. 'My best blue! How can I get rid of this stuff?' he asked in despair. 'My mother used to remove tar with butter – but I doubt if the cookhouse will supply you; I think a dry-cleaners' is your best bet' I advised him, trying to prevent my concerned expression from turning into a broad grin. I bade him goodnight – but paused a moment to watch the slight figure weave its way along the deserted lane into the gathering summer dusk.

Just before lunch the next day, F/Lt Sugden answered a telephone call in Control. 'What? – Who?' a pause. 'Yes – there is.' He turned and grinned at me: 'I think this is someone who wants to speak to you – it's a Canadian and he wants to know if there's a pretty girl with dark hair and big brown eyes on duty!' He held out the receiver to me, and my cheeks flamed under the knowing smiles of the rest of the Control staff. 'You should not phone me on duty!' I said primly into the mouthpiece. 'I'm sorry but I wanted to see you again – may I meet you when you come off duty?' I agreed, mainly to bring the conversation to an end. 'I guess I ought to warn you about these Canadians!' said F/Lt Sugden, solemnly. So it was that I came to know Johnnie, and along with him, the rest of his crew. I told Johnnie about Mike, so that there should be no misunderstandings. Johnnie had a girl back home, so that evened things up. As a companion, he was great fun – sensitive, and quietly humorous. Sometimes we went out together to Lincoln, sometimes with other members of his crew accompanying us – perhaps Wally, who was English – tall, gentle, and with a sweet, quiet smile; or Fin, the mid-upper gunner – Canadian, with a sharp, intelligent face. Or yet another 'Mac' – short and stocky, a French-Canadian, with a shock of black, wiry hair; he was the rear-gunner. Cockney Eddie, the flight-engineer, sometimes came too. Poor Johnnie – he was teased endlessly about his best blue trousers, until the cleaners finally restored them to him – tar-free at last! He had been very sensitive about wearing his oil-stained battledress trousers, which wouldn't hold a crease, and it was something to celebrate when he could leave camp feeling respectable once more. We didn't see much of Johnnie's pilot, or Rick, the navigator, as both were commissioned. Rick, anyway, was romantically involved with one of the Met assistants from our hut – Pat, the possessor of the gramophone.

Going on duty one evening, I met Wally and Mac, the gunner,

returning from a visit to one of the pubs in Bardney village. Wally was more than a foot taller than Mac, who was barely my height; nothing about Wally betrayed the fact that he had been imbibing, except the sparkle in his eye and the dignified deliberation in his gait, but Mac tottered all over the road, with only Wally's restraining hand holding his to keep him from falling. Mac's hair seemed to be standing up straighter than usual, unlike its owner. They looked for the entire world like a dignified father helping along a small son who hadn't quite yet learned to walk, and I exploded into helpless laughter at the sight. Wally just smiled his sweet smile and looked serenely happy, and I don't think Mac even noticed, as they pursued their unsteady course to the Sergeants' Mess.

Ops came and went, how easy to say – Hamburg, Spezia, Wuppertal, Peenemunde, Remscheid – some familiar faces disappeared, to our sorrow and new ones replaced them. 'Window', the radar-confusing strips of metal foil which Cecil had shown me last year, was finally being used, with considerable success we heard. When ops were on and I was off-duty, I joined a little crowd of airmen and WAAF at the beginning of the runway. No one minded this custom at Bardney and as each aircraft taxied round and paused before lumbering off down the concrete to become airborne, we all waved madly, our good wishes flying like a flock of invisible birds alongside. It was as though we wanted to give an extra lift to each pair of wings.

A most fervent demonstration of this desire took place in Control one evening during take off. The runway in use ran almost directly across the airfield in front of the Watch Office so, sitting at my set, I had a good view. Charles, in T-Tare, rumbled along, weighted heavily with bombs, and the Lancaster began to lift as she drew level with the Watch Office. Then, directly opposite, the aircraft seemed to stagger, to hang shuddering for a fraction of a second. At least, that is all it could have been but it seemed to go on forever. If Tare had crashed, the consequences to the crew, to all of us in the Watch Office, were only too obvious. The immense surge of will power to keep the loaded machine airborne could be felt, in that moment, as a tangible force emanating from the Watch Office to the aircraft in a concentrated beam. *Very* concentrated. Perhaps it helped, for Charles managed to pull up her nose and labour into the air; but it was a nasty moment for all of us.

We were not destined to have a peaceful night. 'Hello Rudkin, Lobug P-Peter here,' called one of our aircraft, making contact after returning from ops. And at the same moment, an Air Raid Warning Red came through by telephone. Almost at once, we heard desynchronised engines overhead as the enemy aircraft swooped low across the airfield. Thank God no one was landing, I thought. A spattering, crackling noise followed the path of engine sound, then was gone. The intruder disappeared into the darkness. Just a nuisance raid, but our Canadian FCO suspected anti-personnel bombs – the dangerous little butterfly bombs – had been dropped. The whole incident was over in seconds but now there was nothing for it but to check that the runway and perimeter were clear since we had several aircraft circling, and calls were frequent: 'Rudkin, Lobug L-Love here, when may we land?' Rudkin could only say 'Stand by.' F/Lt Sugden put on his cap and strode out of the room and downstairs, to where the Utility waited outside. The airfield lighting was switched on, and with hearts in mouths, we watched the faint beams from the van's headlights creeping along the perimeter track and then turning on to the runway. For the second time that night, all our psychic energies – if such they could be called – were concentrated on one target. We knew that the vanwheel had only to touch one of the deadly little bombs. But the headlights continued along the runway and back along the perimeter and within a few minutes our FCO was safely back in Control, announcing that the runway was clear and it was OK to start landing. Despite his perilous drive he was calm and collected, and I greatly admired his courage.

Later, when the aircraft were all safely down and the early dawn of summer was lightening the sky, I told him so. The black eyebrows shot up and down. There were shadows under the eyes – but he grinned. 'All part of the job,' he replied, continuing to munch the welcome slices of toast between swallows of cocoa, which Bobby, the young airman who helped around Control, had just brought in. We were all warned to watch our step in the vicinity of the airfield for a while; the intruder's calling cards were still around.

The 'Dig for Victory' campaign was in full swing, and the Flying Control officers decided they would contribute by starting a vegetable garden. Accordingly a patch was dug over near the Watch Office, and it provided an absorbing hobby. Eventually it provided some successful spring onions, and one evening, F/Lt Sugden brought a bunch up to Control and handed them around. I didn't care for raw onion with no accompaniment – but I couldn't spoil his obvious pride in the fruits of his labour by refusing. Afterwards I wished I had. The flavour was so strong that my eyes watered, and I tasted onions with *everything* for days. Onions with porridge or onions with jam was not to my taste – but I got it anyway. I politely refused further offers.

After a few weeks, the Gardening Club became more ambitious – and voted to keep geese. The Flare Party was set to work constructing a shed and pen – with considerable binding on their part – and a small flock of geese was procured, after obtaining permission from the CO. The care of the geese also devolved mainly on the Flare Party; they had to ensure that the birds were secure in their pen when flying was in progress, to avoid casualties. The geese rather resented their loss of freedom however, and occasionally staged an escape – causing a large-scale flap until they were rounded up. It was not an uncommon sight to see them waddling along the perimeter track in line astern as though this was their exclusive right-of-way – only to turn flapping and honking, all dignity gone, when faced with a Lancaster taxiing towards them. Depending on the pilot concerned, the R/T would occasionally explode into life: 'Get those bloody birds out of my way!' Others were more or less polite. Eventually, after providing us with many laughs, they became too much, and their banishment was decreed. I suspect they ended up on the dinner table of the Officers' Mess.

Incredibly, Johnnie and I found ourselves on extraordinarily good terms with the Station SPs – usually a detested breed! We never quite worked out how it happened, but coming back on the evening bus from Lincoln, we had only to appear at the Guardroom, and were instantly invited in for a cup of tea and made welcome there. We often puzzled about it. It was nothing less than astonishing. A similar situation arose for me at Sick Quarters. I visited the MO over a minor health concern, and there met Charlie, Bill and Bert, the pipe-smoking corporal-medical orderly. They were a friendly bunch, and the MO was nice; he was young, and rather delicate-looking I thought. Greatly daring, I took my camera round to Sick Quarters and asked if I could photograph them all. Obligingly, they posed by the ambulance. 'Make sure you get the Red Cross in the picture,' said Doc, anxiously. I did, and the resulting photos were quite good; at least, they all wanted copies. I was invited round to SSQ to share supper with the orderlies occasionally after this – perhaps they thought I needed building up. Extra portions were scrounged from the cookhouse, and I enjoyed these bukshee meals. There was nothing wrong with my appetite; a dish of real eggs and baked beans was not to be missed, and sometimes there would be a rasher of bacon too – this was luxury! Tea at the Guardroom, supper at Sick Quarters – how could I be so lucky? I concluded it was just that Bardney was that sort of station.

It was a lovely summer. The sun shone warmly, and the trees and hedges were lush and heavy with midsummer growth. Great banks of willow herb thrust up purple-pink spires round the concrete hardstandings where the Lancasters were dispersed on the edges of conifer plantations, dark and aromatic. Overall was the bowl of blue air, sometimes there were clouds, too, but as I wrote in a letter to Jo, now posted from 44 to the new squadron, 619, at Woodhall Spa: 'I have invented a new occupation – cloud-watching. One lies on one's back on the grass, and simply gazes above – some very beautiful effects are to be observed!' And so there were. My spirits were lighter than for some time, and Johnnie's companionship was a boon. I cared a great deal about him, but I wasn't in love with him… or perhaps I was, just a little. If so, neither of us spoke about it. But I was in love with life; it seemed good – uncomplicated and happy.

I had a leave. At home, a friend of my mother's had a spaniel puppy left out of a litter her dog had produced, and she allowed me to take him for walks. I christened him Ropey and adored him. I knew I couldn't keep him. Living over a shop was not a good habitat for a dog, and my mother had enough to do in my absence; in any case, she wasn't fit enough to look after a demanding small dog. I pretended he was mine though for my leave, and sent a postcard to Johnnie telling him all about Ropey. He replied that he envied me, and wished he could be along when I was walking Ropey – and asked me to let him know the train I'd be back on; if he wasn't 'dicing', he'd meet me. He was tired of talking to himself after a week of it. There were letters from Mike too. He wasn't a prolific letter-writer, and the spontaneity seemed to be going out of our correspondence. I wondered, but continued to write. There was a lack of reality about our relationship – and I knew it was my own fault, if I forced myself to consider it. Mostly, I side-stepped the issue. Joan and I made a few excursions to Dunholme Lodge, to see John – to whom she was now engaged – and Mac and Tim and Norman. Not many of the Gang were left now, but it was lovely to see those who were. Then John was posted to Fiskerton, and there wasn't really a Gang any more. I continued to keep in touch with Mac and Tim by letter and heard occasional news of others through them. I didn't see much of Joan off duty any more, as her outings were now to Fiskerton whenever possible.

I wrote to Sally frequently and, now and then, she came over to Bardney on the transport to see me. Not often though, as most of her off-duty time was committed to the new Waddo dramatic society. She was a natural actress and, with her appealing looks, had the lead role more often than not, so she was kept busy. Still, there was to be a dance in the Sergeants' Mess. Johnnie had invited me, and suggested I ask Sally along too. She had promised to come, and I went to meet her off the 17.30 transport that evening. I waited and waited, but there was no sign of it. Enquiries at the Guardroom drew a blank – they knew nothing of it except that it hadn't appeared. I went off to have tea and get ready for the dance. We were to meet Johnnie at 20.00 in the Mess; perhaps she would arrive on the later transport at 19.30. Once more I waited at the Guardroom, and this time the transport did appear, and with it, the story behind the non-arrival of the previous one. There had been an accident – a collision in which both vehicles were badly damaged – and there had been some casualties. The driver couldn't tell me more than that and, thoroughly worried, I went off to ring the Waafery to see if there was any news of Sally. She was in WAAF sick-bay, shocked and badly bruised, but not seriously damaged. I thanked heaven it was no worse; I was still anxious to know what happened, but I wasn't to hear all the details for a few days. With my mind a little easier, I went on to the Sergeants' Mess where Johnnie was waiting – I was late, and flustered. It took me a little while to settle down and enjoy it, but Johnnie, Fin and Mac soon had me dancing. I swayed with Johnnie to 'That Ol' Black Magic', and it began to seem appropriate...but no, I wouldn't think in those terms.

Eventually I heard Sally's story of the accident. She had been about to get into the back of the transport with a number of airmen also coming to Bardney. A lot of W/T gear had already been loaded inside. F/O Sanson, the junior Signals Officer, was climbing into the driver's cab, and seeing Sally, whom he knew, called to her to come and sit in the front, which she did as there was plenty of room. 'As usual,' she said ruefully, 'I hadn't booked out.' The vehicle drove out towards the Sleaford road and was in the process of turning on to it, when a police car came racing along at high speed, and apparently was unable to brake in time; it smashed into the transport with considerable impact. Sally saw, in a split second, what was about to happen and screamed, though had no recollection of it. Her next memory was of lying on the grass verge of the road, with F/O Sanson leaning over her, his mouth bleeding badly with two front teeth missing and upper lip swelling; he asked her if she was hurt. On trying to reply, Sally found her voice would not come. She tried again, explaining in a forced, hoarse whisper that she had lost her voice. She said afterwards that she would never forget how, even in that moment of shock, F/O Sanson tried to smile, despite the painful injuries to his mouth saying: 'Never mind, we will look for it afterwards!'

After this, Sally lay where she was for a few minutes, slowly coming to the realisation that at least no bones were broken. She sat up cautiously and looked around, discovering that her uniform was torn and covered in oil. She saw that the lorry was overturned and the W/T sets from inside it were scattered all over the road and injured airmen lay in varying stages of consciousness. Miraculously, out of nowhere, somebody appeared with a pail of water and bandages, which Sally proceeded to apply where they seemed most needed. The driver had a great gash to the bone in his leg: 'It wasn't even bleeding – I just slapped some cotton wool and a bandage over it before I had time to think about it,' she told me. The worst case she did her best to help and comfort was that of a man from the RAF Regiment, lying in the middle of the road, with both hands terribly cut, blood streaming down his face from one eye, and a deep gash in his head. When the ambulance finally arrived – 'It seemed like hours' – Sally was sitting with his head in her lap, still in the middle of the road, wiping the blood from his eyes and saying over and over, 'Nevermind, love, you'll be all right.' Her turn came to get into the ambulance, and she was told to lie down, though insisting she was perfectly all right. By the time she arrived at WAAF Sick Bay, she had begun to feel not at all right – in fact, shaky, sick, and bruised. A large bump on her head was the obvious cause of a raging headache; she was quite badly concussed. She also had a deep cut on her arm and a bruise covering most of her thigh, as well as other minor cuts and bruises, so she had certainly not escaped the crash unscathed. I deeply admired the way she had coped with the situation and sights which, the mere thought of, left me shuddering with horror.

There was a court case later, about the cause of the accident, and she was called as a witness. The lawyers tried hard to establish that either F/O Sanson or the driver had spoken to, or touched her immediately before the collision, and thus had their attention off the road. This had not been the case and her reply, in its transparent innocence and honesty, made the judge smile, and sent a ripple of laughter through the court. It must have been what later became known as a 'Sally-ism'! The case was dismissed.

Italian cities, as well as German cities, had for some time been among the targets for our bombers. Now came the 'shuttle-raids', in which the aircraft bombed an Italian target, flew on to a base in North Africa, refuelled and bombed-up again in preparation for another attack on the return flight. Three 9 Squadron crews were detailed for one of these raids in mid-July. The CO, W/Cdr Burnett, was flying, as was Johnnie's crew. The target on the outward flight was Reggio nell' Emilia, not a name most of us were familiar with. Johnnie was quite looking forward to the African stopover. He promised to come up to Control some time in the evening to say cheerio as I was on duty until midnight, and take-off was at 22.00 hrs. He was flying in WS-P. When his head appeared round the door, it seemed reasonable to go and make some tea and have a few words with Johnnie in private.

The raid, he said, should be a piece of cake, and he would bring me some bananas back from Africa! We continued chatting for a short while longer, but the time was getting on: 'Well – guess I'd better be going – see you in three days' time!' he smiled. But the smile changed and twisted, as the same thought knifed through both our minds at that moment. There would be no meeting in three days – perhaps ever – my flash of foreknowledge didn't extend that far. We stood stunned and motionless for seconds. Then Johnnie reached out for me and kissed me, his lips hard on mine. It was a kiss of parting, and we both knew it. He turned and left quickly and still neither of us had spoken. What was there to say?

When take-off started, I watched P-Peter's departure. How was Johnnie feeling, after that dreadful premonition we had both experienced? Like me probably, trying to convince himself that it was just imagination – that it wouldn't happen. The inevitable news came next day. The other two aircraft had landed safely in North Africa. Johnnie's aircraft had gone down over Northern Italy. I could feel no worse than I already did; it was merely confirmation of what I knew inwardly in spite of my efforts to reject it. Whether Johnnie and the rest of the crew were alive or dead, I dared not contemplate. All I knew was that, once missing, aircrew rarely reappeared, and much of the light and brilliance disappeared from the summer, switched off like the beam of a torch on a dark night.

I remembered that he told me the crew had had their photo taken at a studio in Lincoln just a few days previously – defying a superstition that a crew did not have a photograph taken as a group until their tour was complete. I made up my mind to search for the photographer's shop and get some copies of the photograph. On my next afternoon off, I set about my quest. It took time, and visits to half-a-dozen or more shops before I found the one I was seeking – and I still couldn't order any prints I was told, without a chit from the Station Adjutant confirming that the crew was missing. This I obtained from a sympathetic Adjutant, and was then able to place an order. The photos, when I collected them, showed a rather stiff little group of seven, some smiling, or half-smiling, and some serious. Johnnie was one of these. I wondered if this was the only way I'd ever see him now – looking out of a photograph?

I decided quite suddenly to write to his mother. I described how we'd met, and the friendship we'd so briefly shared, and about the few moments before he left to go on this ill-fated trip. I tried to keep in mind that there was a girlfriend back in Canada, and that the letter would most probably be shown to her. I didn't want anyone to feel more cause for grief than must surely already be the case. The Orderly Room gave me the address, and I enclosed the photo and airmailed the letter. Johnnie's mother replied quickly. She said my letter had been 'the answer to a prayer'. She had so longed to hear from someone who knew him and could tell her of his life in this country, as he so rarely mentioned details – just said he was well, everything was fine, and not to worry. She told me of her large family, and one son killed whilst serving with the Canadian Navy and how they all hoped and prayed that Johnnie was safe. She herself felt that he was and she begged me to write again; I continued to do so, glad that I had followed my impulse to contact her.

There was some solace to be found, cycling solitarily around the neighbouring countryside. The land, though fairly flat, was well-wooded, and I loved the shady lanes overhung with tree branches and dappled with sunlight, and the broad fields shimmering with ripening grain. Once a great flock of starlings circled above me, spreading out, gaining height, and filling the sky with a susurration of wings – black flickering shapes against the whiteness of towering cumulus cloud. In the little time-untouched Lincolnshire villages there were small grey churches which I liked to stop at and explore.

Bardney village was pleasant enough, but fairly unremarkable. No one told me that it had been the site of one of the greatest Benedictine Abbeys in Europe! Perhaps because there was nothing left to see except bumps and dips in a field. On the outskirts of the village the River Witham flowed, much frequented in the summer months by bathers and fishermen. One hot August afternoon, I decided to try swimming there myself. I wore my swimsuit under my uniform and divested myself of tunic, skirt and shirt behind a convenient bush. Treading gingerly through the long grass, I reached the water's edge – and found I didn't relish the sensation of soft mud seeping between my toes as I stepped into the water. I launched myself forward and started to swim, and the cool water against my hot skin was blissful; that is, until I sensed something brushing gently against me from below, something twining around my arms and legs as they moved through the water.

I saw that I was over a wide band of water-weed, and it seemed that the dark green undulating fronds were trying to trap me with their soft, persistent clutch. As usual, my imagination was working overtime but for a few seconds, I felt real panic – even lost my rhythm and found myself splashing and struggling. I mastered my fright and kicked away from the weed without too much delay, swimming towards the opposite bank of the river. A bleached and rotting barge lay derelict there, half full of water, and I hung on to its side, panting a little until I felt calmer. And when I did I wanted to get out of the water; but it meant braving that horrible weed again. I wished that I were a stronger swimmer – or a more fearless one. I let go my hold on the barge and swam slowly and deliberately back, trying to ignore the dark, sinister caress of the weed as I passed over it. It couldn't possibly have dragged me down to a watery grave – it just felt like it. In a moment my feet were on the muddy bank and I made rapidly for my bush, praying that no one had stolen my clothes – that really would finish off my afternoon. But no, there they were, and I lost no time drying myself and getting into them. Well, at least I was cooler. But it seemed that rivers and I did not agree: first, the episode of the boat at Brayford Pool, and now this. Swimming baths for me in future I thought.

I had a 48-hour pass coming up, and didn't want to go home. I'd go somewhere I hadn't been before! I chose Stratford-on-Avon. I did go home first, to collect my 'civvies', and to say hello to my parents, then caught a train onwards. I found a hotel which looked comfortable, and 10/– for bed and breakfast didn't seem too expensive. Then I set out to explore Stratford and was enchanted with it. The little streets of half-timbered cottages and grander, stone houses; Shakespeare's birthplace, the Guild Chapel, the Parish Church, Harvard House and, of course, the theatre! My only disappointment was that the Summer Season programme didn't include Shakespeare's plays, and I had so much wanted to see one.

But I was happy with all that I saw of the town – and very surprised, on my second day, to run into Jack, a sergeant-pilot, who had been one of our Control odd bods at Waddington for a short while. He had been awaiting posting then, and was now at an OTU near Stratford. His new crew was with him and he invited me to join them all for tea. We trooped into a restaurant, and Jack and I caught up on events since his departure from Waddington as we ate. He commented that he had scarcely recognised me out of uniform, in my green Harris Tweed suit, and hair caught back in a snood. I noticed a difference in him too. When with us in Control, he had still seemed a boy, drawing (very well) pictures of aircraft to amuse himself when no other occupation offered. Now, suddenly, he was assured and responsible. Having a crew of his own and learning to fly as its skipper had clearly changed him. I wished him well when we parted and, privately, all the luck in the world.

I looked forward to going to see Ann Hathaway's Cottage, thatched and bedecked with roses like the postcards, and found I'd need to take a short bus ride. I should, of course, have asked to be told when we reached the stop, but thought I would be sure to recognise it. Somehow, I didn't and was confounded to see I'd arrived back in Stratford, where I boarded the bus in the first place. I sidled off the bus feeling very foolish, certain that the conductor was having a smirk at my expense. I never did get to see it as I was leaving in the morning. But all in all, it had been a very worth while journey. When I got home, to put on my uniform again – a letter from the Canadian Red Cross awaited me. I had contacted them for news of Johnnie, should there be any, and now learned that he was a POW in Italy. So at least he was alive! They had no address yet – but the news that he had survived was cause enough for rejoicing.

As soon as I got back to camp, I wrote to his mother. Her reply told me joyfully that they had received the good news and she enclosed a cutting from their local paper about Johnnie, which included the announcement that he had been awarded the DFM. I felt very proud of him, and more light-hearted than for some weeks past. But it was many months before more definite news was forthcoming.

The board for our LACW was due to take place in early autumn and the other R/T ops and I had been poring over our gen-books. As we were on three watches and also having to go over to Waddington for instruction each week, usually after coming off night duty, we decided on a joint protest. We were all very tired, and the situation was hardly ideal. Waddo Control was not on three watches, and moreover, had had a quiet summer with little or no flying so we felt a little temporary assistance from them would be helpful. Three R/T operators went to see the SFCO – the one, I was still convinced, who did not like me. But he was the boss. We stood in front of his desk. 'Well?' he said. No one spoke. I took the plunge; it seemed as if no one else was going to. I explained what seemed to us a very unfair situation in relation to our studies, since we had less time to gen up and we were very tired and, warming to my subject, said it was ridiculous to expect us to cope well under these circumstances if no extra help was forthcoming. The others were by now standing well behind me, and still no one else said a word. 'You think so?' said the SFCO, a little truculently. 'Yes, sir, I do.' We left Control with no promise of extra staff and no encouragement of any kind, and grumbling broke out afresh. I didn't say any more. There didn't seem much point; we'd obviously just have to put up with it. It would have been nice to have a little more support, though.

The board duly arrived and somehow we all passed. Among other technicalities, we had to signal and receive Morse by Aldis lamp at six words per minute – something which could only be practised satisfactorily after dark. At least we had something to show for this we thought, as, happily, we sewed 'props' badges on to our tunic sleeves. It also provided some welcome extra cash too. *And* we had succeeded in spite of difficulties, so could afford to feel just a little smug at our achievement. The only annoyance was that Waddington's SFCO had proved himself right to take no action on our behalf!

I began to talk to Grace, our radar mechanic/acting R/T operator, when we were in the hut on our own. She had her own circle of friends, and was engaged and soon to be married to Sergeant Jack Dickinson, another Canadian WOp/AG. He was tall, lanky and easy going. Grace, tiny and pretty in a completely natural fashion, with an aura of fascination about her which was hard to pin down. It had to do with her love of nature and her vivid imagination, and her appreciation of the imagination of others. We found we were both reading the same books – books by Mary Webb and Joan Grant – and to each of us they opened up vistas only half suspected previously, in richness of imagery and colour.

She and Jack spent their honeymoon in her grandmother's cottage in the Lake District, where it had rained often, but, she said, they had gone out walking whatever the weather, enjoying the wonderful views in turn concealed, then revealed by the veils of cloud. On their last complete day the weather cleared, and they watched a glorious sunset from the hillside on which the cottage stood. Grace described it so that I almost saw her irradiated by the brilliance of colour and light in that western sky, and she retained within herself some of its magic.

There were conversations, too, with Audrey and Pat from the Met Office. These were always lively and interesting and both were charming girls: Audrey, sunny and even-tempered; Pat, more serious – moody sometimes but never discourteous, whatever her feelings. She and I were both on our knees, polishing our bed spaces one morning when she burst forth, evidently having had the subject on her mind for a while, 'You know, it really is *too* bad the way the WAAF are not taken seriously. So many people seem to consider we are here for one purpose only – to get a man! Yet I joined up with very deep feelings about what I was doing, and they had nothing to do with men!' A sentiment I totally understood. Undeniably, the boyfriends were there – as I supposed they would have been even without a war for our age-group; but for the majority of us they had not been our reason for joining the forces. Those of us who had volunteered had, in general, been motivated by the wish – the need even – to take an active part in the war, and to do something useful. We bitterly resented the labels pinned thoughtlessly onto us as a whole, of 'Aircrew Comforts, Officers, for the use of', and other such derogatory descriptions. We comforted ourselves with the thought that those who knew us would not subscribe to these views. Yet we knew many people – like Gerry, the pilot I had met at home, and then so briefly when I arrived at Waddington – who held that we were all tarred with the same brush. It seemed most unfair.

The Station church was in the Nissen hut next to Hut 6. Waddington's padre came over to take services, and had to get his organist as and where he could find one. Tim was always a standby for him, but it meant a journey from Dunholme Lodge, which Tim didn't mind too much as he now had his own little sports car. He drove over one Sunday to play for morning service – a circumstance I knew nothing of, as it had been a last minute arrangement. In any case, I had been on duty all night and had just dropped off to sleep. I was awakened – rudely I considered – by sounds of the organ, and singing, for which I wasn't at all in the mood. I was very tired – so tired that I was almost in tears at having my sleep snatched from me – and I became more and more fretful and irritable as the service progressed. I was wide awake when it ended, and when I thought the congregation would have dispersed and the hut would be empty (except for the padre and the wretched organist, whoever he might be) I got out of bed, flung on my dressing gown, and marched round to the church, tousle-haired and sleepy-eyed. Tim and the padre were packing up, ready to leave, and stared at me in some astonishment. I knew I was being irrational, but I couldn't stop myself; I held forth on the lack of consideration in waking up people who'd been on night duty, especially after a busy ops night, with 'all the noise' – I was quite beside myself. Although it was dear old 'Tim of the Gang' – the choral society and the concert party – I was unable to restrain my tirade until exhaustion took over, which didn't take long.

The padre gently apologised, whilst Tim said nothing – just gazed at me. I glared at him and left. It was only later that extreme embarrassment and discomfiture overtook me – how *could* I have made such a scene? I felt dreadful.

Autumn drew on. There was a stand-down of almost two weeks because of poor weather. I sat, night duty after night duty, in a half-lit Control room, watching the field-mice play about the floor and run over the bench, as they did when all was quiet. The nights had grown chilly, and they enjoyed the warmth of the heating pipes as much as I did. On one such night, after a couple of hours of writing letters and studying French grammar, which I'd returned to, I dragged an armchair round near the pipes and wrapped myself in a blanket, as was common practice on nights of no flying, and dozed fitfully, every crackle from the loudspeaker registering in my brain. A human voice, however faint, awoke me in an instant – a state of awareness in R/T operators, and very necessary. I was startled when, at around 03.00 hrs, the Control office door burst open, and in strode F/Lt Sugden. Seeing me wrapped in my blanket and reclining by the hot water pipes, he strode round the bench, and his reply to my 'Hello, sir?' was to accuse me of sleeping on duty, and a threat to put me on a charge. 'Get round to that set and stay there!' he snapped, walking out before I could offer a word of explanation. I supposed that in his eyes, there *was* no explanation – but I was desperately upset as I knew with certainty that no 'Darky' call would have gone unheard – and furthermore, this was not the F/Lt Sugden I was accustomed to. He seemed a different person.

I burst into tears. Bobby, the 18-year-old Control assistant, who heard what had taken place whilst coming upstairs, came in.

'Don't cry, Pip,' he said, his large brown eyes sympathetic and anxious. 'I'll get you some cocoa.' I drank it, tears still dripping down my face. I had never, ever been accused of neglect of duty before, and it went against all my training and discipline, and the pride I had in my job. I wept again, disconsolately, and poor Bobby didn't know what to do to comfort me, except to sit with me. I had pulled myself together by morning, but poured it all out unhappily to Grace, when I saw her in the hut. 'Oh, don't worry about it,' she said reassuringly, 'he'd probably been to a party in the Mess and had a few drinks, and then got depressed. He's like that sometimes. You'll hear no more about it.' True enough – I didn't. It was never mentioned again.

I began to feel restless and not sure what I wanted; a change of some sort, but what? A new WAAF trade was advertised in DROs – that of Radar Mechanic (Air). It meant that one was trained to service radar sets and flew on air tests to try them out – officially. I still wanted to fly in spite of my earlier disasters. Hopefully I'd get used to it, I thought, if I passed the course. So I applied to remuster, after talking to some of the other radar mechs. In due course I had to report to Padgate for a trade test. What a depressing place it was! I had never seen anywhere quite so cheeerless, dank, and dreary. I hated it the moment I set foot in the camp. It seemed to set the seal of doom on my venture before it had even started. After the inevitable, endless sessions of waiting about, the various tests were completed, and again I waited to hear the result. I had failed. My maths had let me down. I really should have known – they never were my strong point. I pleaded in vain that I'd study to get my maths up to the required standard before the course started. No dice. The biggest blow was that as I'd chosen to remuster and failed the test for the radar mechanics' course I would be sent on a wireless operators course! Apparently I'd done well in the Morse aptitude test I'd taken without thinking about it, and WAAF W/Ops were being recruited just then.

I found Morse worrying, though I'd been conversant with it – to a certain extent – from my youthful Girl Guide days, and particularly since there had been a necessity to know it for my

R/T boards. There had been my recent Aldis lamp practice – no wonder I'd done well in the aptitude test! But I had no ambitions as regards wireless operating. The Signals Officer at Bardney did his best to get me off the hook, but all his efforts were to no avail, I had to go. I was to leave at the beginning of November – destination, Blackpool. 'You lucky thing – you'll have a wonderful time there!' various people said, on hearing the news. But I didn't want to go to Blackpool. I now realised I wanted to stay at Bardney. Well, I should have considered that before setting these ponderous forces in motion, I supposed ruefully as I packed my kitbag.

Pip Beck

The Watch Office, RAF Waddington.

Joyce Rogers, Pip's friend with whom
she joined up

Sally, who became Pip's friend.

II

Pip (right) and Sally in Flying Control on a night of no flying.

A busy night on the Watch Office roof.

Hampden aircraft from 44 Squadron.

A 207 Squadron Avro Manchester.

The Rhodesians' Christmas dance, Assembly Rooms Lincoln, 1941.
Pip Beck to the left of the two talking Sergeants, 2nd row from front.

The Horse and Jockey pub, Waddington village.

A 44 Squadron Avro Lancaster, flown by Squadron Leader Nettleton VC.

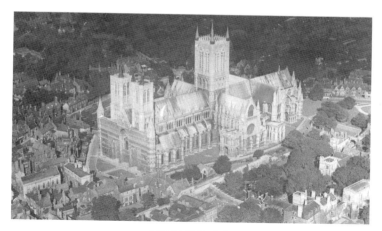

Lincoln Cathedral.

An Oxford aircraft.

9 Squadron, Bardney Flying Control.
Joan Herbert at R/T, with Squadron Leader Shobrook.

Station Sick Quarters with
Charlie, Doc Wright and
Bill.

Crew of 'P' Peter, 9 Squadron. Back L to R Finn, Johnny Merchant, Mac, Eddie.
Front L to R, Wally, 'Mac' Head and Dick.

Maureen who accompanied Pip
Beck from Bridgnorth to
Waddington.

'Brim' who became Pip's husband.

The Watch Office, Upper Heyford.

Joyce's wedding to Derek Crooks(RAAF), 1944. Pip Beck as bridesmaid.

7

Blackpool Nights

The syllables 'Black-pool' rang like a knell in my brain. I had endured a long, grey, cramped train journey from Lincoln, during which the dullness of the morning had deepened into a dim afternoon of low cloud and drizzle. And I was getting a cold. By the time the train pulled into Blackpool Central it was dark and pouring with rain. I reported to the RTO and was told to join a group of pinch-faced WAAF on the platform who, it transpired, were also posted to Course 2IE, I3 Radio School, the course I was to reluctantly join myself. Our miserable little group waited. We were used to that. But the station was full of needling draughts. One or two tried to light cigarettes but the wind got there first, blowing out the match flames. 'Where the *hell* is the transport?' moaned someone. I felt like crying.

Transport turned up, and took us to our allotted billets. Most of us were dropped off at a tall, narrow boarding house in Hornby Road. We were assembled in the lounge cum dining-room, where our landlady rapidly made it apparent to us that she would have preferred airmen to WAAF. We were to behave ourselves and not cause her any trouble, and she didn't want any 'dirty habits' – on this she didn't specify. We didn't take to her either. She was shapeless and colourless. I was to share a tiny box of a room with a girl called Joyce. Thankfully, we liked each other immediately, which was fortunate since we were to live in such close proximity. Two beds filled most of the space, and they were not full length. My 5ft 2in touched top and bottom of the bed, and it was lucky for Joyce that she was no taller. I wondered if Blackpool had a factory producing extra-short beds for extra-short rooms!

During the first few days, I felt displaced and woebegone and my cold grew worse. I desperately missed the green fields of Bardney, and longed for aircraft on runways instead of the streets and traffic of this place. Our days started with a cold wash at the basin in our room. We had no such luxuries as hot water. I was relieved to find that we got hot showers at the

Derby Baths, to which we were marched once a week.

I felt sure all Blackpool landladies were not alike – but ours could have been improved on. Breakfast was meagre. We never got our butter rations – the family downstairs must have consumed the lot. The tea came already milked, though not a lot, in a giant enamel teapot. After we'd eaten, we dashed out to a nearby street corner where a WAAF corporal paraded us, called the roll by the light of a street lamp, and marched us off to Olympia, still in the dark. And it rained!

At first, Olympia seemed full of Morse code signals – di di di dah dah, di dah di di, di di dah – groups of letters, groups of numbers, drumming through our earphones. No plain language in which the identification of a few letters helped in guessing a word. Each symbol needed to be recognised. The hall, huge and echoing, began to take on dreamlike proportions. Sometimes, I did dream about it and found myself looking down from the spaces of the lofty roof, filled with dust and shadows. Grey motes of dust absorbed any light that entered. Sunlight through a window was not allowed in my dream. The dust-motes smothered it. Far below, little blue-clad figures hummed and buzzed inadequately among themselves, as they did in reality, under the stern eye of a grey-haired warrant officer wearing a navigator's brevet. He had rimless glasses and carried a short cane for rapping on tables. I kept my eyes lowered when he was around, terrified in case he divined my faltering comprehension. We looked forward eagerly to morning and afternoon breaks, being ever hungry. There were cafés which catered specially for us but our favourite was Woolworths, next to the Tower. The whole class made for it, desperate to get to the counter in time to purchase the delicious little pancakes we loved. Afterwards, it was off to another lecture room. There were many dotted around the streets of central Blackpool, behind or above shops or club rooms like the one in which we received instruction in procedure and technical knowledge. The windows were velvet-curtained still, and it smelled faintly of cigars and wine. No doubt Blackpool businessmen had congregated here to spend some of their brass. Now we were here, sitting in rows on hard chairs and taking down the information our sergeant-instructor wrote on a blackboard, hoping we could make sense of it.

Wednesday afternoons and Sundays were free. It was then that I set out to explore, glad to see daylight for an uninterrupted few hours. I loved it when the wind came in from the sea and the waves smashed against the sea wall, sending cascades of spray over the promenade and scattering unwary walkers. The brown water, veined with creamy foam, sucked back then surged forward again, curling up in a great crescent. I waited for it to break, timing my run past the point of greatest impact to avoid a drenching. Salt water and sea air ruined the polish on uniform buttons. They needed cleaning at least twice a day, though mine were not always so lucky, but the sight of the waves was worth a few extra minutes with the Brasso. There were other things to do if the weather was impossible. New plays were given a preliminary run in Blackpool, and I made the most of this opportunity to see them before they reached the West End. I was enthralled by *They Came to a City*, by Emlyn Williams. The whole of the action took place on the side of a hill, and the story moved along in changes of lighting – dawn, full sun, evening, night – translucent, brilliant, magical and mysterious. It was like the light and colour of a dream, and it continued to glow in my memory.

A group of girls from our billet went occasionally to dances at the Tower Ballroom, and I went with them. The Ballroom seemed enormous, full of light, music and voices, cigarette smoke creating a blue haze above. A vast, pulsing throng of dancers filled the floor and we became a part of it, dancing with an airman or a soldier, a Pole or an American, moving to the rhythmic beat of the orchestra as if in a trance.

Evelyn created a diversion one evening. She, a tall Canadian girl from our billet, fainted dramatically in the middle of the dance floor, causing a swirl of chaos among the dancers. Her partner gallantly scooped her up and carried her into the foyer, where cooler air revived her. Joyce and I escorted her back to the billet. Our landlady, on hearing what had happened, grudgingly produced a cup of tea for Evelyn – though not for us – but gave her a sharp look from small, pale eyes. Every line on her face expressed suspicion. Later, ready to gloat, she asked me, 'She's not – pregnant – is she?' 'No,' I said shortly. Evelyn would have been furious at the suggestion, and I didn't tell her. She disliked our landlady enough as it was. An American saw me back to Hornby Road after another dance. I had earlier made up my mind that there would be no American dates for me. Everyone else seemed to go out with them. I thought I would be different. Anyway, I didn't like the tiresome brashness most Americans displayed. This man, though, was different. He was quiet with an accent less obvious than most. Lean, dark haired, with an angular, bony face, he had an air of cultivation. He told me, when we were dancing, that he was a painter. As we walked back from the Tower, he said he would like to paint my portrait. But where? We stood outside by the front door steps, trying to work out how it could be done. In the end, we were defeated. There were no options open. Billets would be hopeless, as would any of the Forces clubs or canteens, so we shrugged, said goodnight and parted. I was disappointed though. I'd always imagined having my portrait in oils hanging on a wall at home, my hair loose and floating!

November was ending. I had a letter from James in reply to an earlier one of mine, in which I had poured out my unhappiness over the posting to Blackpool. I had wailed – and apologised for it. 'Don't ever apologise for writing to me about your troubles. What the hell do you think a friend is for?' he demanded, and I could almost hear his deep, slow voice. He went on to give me advice about how to get myself off the course. '1. Apply for a commission in any damn branch. 2. Plug away at failing the course. Stick at a speed – say, eight words a minute. May not be easy, but it will be worth it in the long run or you'll spend the rest of your service life listening to those bloody dots and dashes! 3. Report sick on every possible occasion – loss of sleep, nerves etc. 4. After two or three weeks of the latter, put in a letter to the CO asking to be taken off the course on health grounds. If there are any difficulties, back it up with a moan to the WAAF CO, and point out that they are still recruiting R/T operators.' And he enclosed a sample letter.

'*Don't* make it too mild, and for God's sake *don't* be too goddamned meek or answer "Yes" when he asks you to carry on and see if things improve! And,' he went on, 'if you're feeling too browned off, just take your headset off, put it on the table, and have a rest. If there's a switch in front of you which will put the ruddy Morse off – SWITCH IT OFF! Failing that, lay a metal pencil or your cap-badge across the terminals of your headset. That'll fix the whole ruddy lot of them. I remember only too well just how deadly it is in the Olympia Hall – especially in November. Is it still as damn cold? Look after yourself, my dear, and get well soon.' (I'd told him about my persistent cold). 'God bless, and if you want a weep-by-correspondence at any time – just get cracking! And write soon anyway.' Dear James! As it happened, I was to see the MO sooner than I expected.

I had been invited to visit an old friend of mine who was staying with her aunt and uncle in Lytham St Anne's. She was recuperating after a rather serious illness. I caught a tram along the front, and found the house easily. A big coal fire burned in the grate and Joan and I sat in armchairs large enough to curl up in on either side of it, chattering happily until teatime. We hadn't seen each other for a very long time. After tea, we returned to our armchairs – vacated, I suspected, by her hospitable aunt and uncle for our benefit – and continued our exchange of news. As the evening passed, I began to feel chilled in spite of the fire. I'd had a cold for so long that I'd grown used to it, but when I began to shiver I realised that something else was setting in – probably 'flu. I said I thought I'd better leave. Joan's aunt looked at me anxiously and tried to persuade me to stay the night, but I refused. I didn't want to leave any more 'flu germs around than I already had, and risk infecting Joan, already low in resistance.

Very reluctantly I went out into the frosty night and caught a tram along the prom. It rattled along in the darkness, the dim light inside causing vague reflections on the windows. I willed it to hurry up and get me back – I was so *cold*. I shivered uncontrollably and my teeth chattered, jarring my aching head. In bed, I still shook, finally falling into a feverish sleep where phantom streams of Morse code clattered through wild dreams. I awoke feeling hot and ill. Joyce told me to stay in bed, promising to explain to our corporal – who came up to take a look at me and said she'd get the MO to call. Amazingly, a cup of tea was brought in by someone. My temperature surged up and fell to the other extreme. I hated Blackpool, hated Morse, hated Hornby Road, and felt worse than ever.

Eventually the MO came, took my temperature, felt my pulse and said, 'Right – we'll have you in sick-bay very shortly.' That was a comfort anyway. What wasn't was having to get up, dress and pack all my belongings. I hoped I'd got everything, but didn't much care if I hadn't. I didn't have the strength to shut my case, and was dazedly trying to sit on it when the medical orderly from the ambulance came up for me. She quickly fastened it and carried it down for me, then I was on my way to the seafront hotel which was now used as a WAAF sick-bay. I was so grateful to get into a comfortable bed – I was even given a hot-water bottle, which was a wonderful comfort, and there were people to look after me.

For several days, I felt too ill to take much notice of my surroundings and I seemed to spend all my nights coughing. I dimly realised that there was another girl in a bed across the room – she also coughed! We were the only two in the small ward. Sometimes I caught a glimpse of a mop of blonde hair above a flushed face, but several days passed before either of us felt like saying 'hello'. When we did, I discovered she was an American – she had come over to this country to join the WAAF and was on a photographic course. She looked so young with her fair curls, blue eyes and pink and white complexion, all of which went with a merry disposition. I thought she couldn't possibly be more than 18. When we got to talking about ourselves, I said she seemed very young to have come over here on her own. She laughed. 'My dear – I have a degree!' she said, which made her at least a year older than me. Her subject had been Art, and we talked of pictures and enjoyed each other's company.

We were allowed up, then down into the common-room. Feeling better but not yet allowed out, we sat there looking out over the sea, almost obscured by mist. We were bored. Energy seemed to be returning and we wanted an occupation. On impulse, we decided to clean the windows! Everyone else thought we were quite mad, but we collected cloths and dusters and set about our self-imposed task with enthusiasm. There were two long side windows and a wide centre window. We took a side each – Pat did the top of the centre window, and I the lower half. Rude comments from the other occupants of the common-room only spurred us on. I suppose it did seem crazy, we were supposed to be ill, so why were we *working*?

But we were rewarded by the view over the sea. The scene we looked out on had the delicacy of a watercolour. The sea had been veiled all day in a thick white mist; now the sun was setting and the mist was pearly, changing to rose and thinning as the sun slipped down behind the sea, placid and silver. Sky was visible – a far, pale blue. We watched the opalescent colours change and fade as we polished the windows, each feeling a sense of quiet fulfilment – and the window *did* look better! Even the other patients agreed when it was done.

After this both Pat and I improved rapidly. There were a few more days at sickbay, during which we now took turns at helping with the washing up in the pokey little hotel kitchen; all almost-better patients were expected to give a hand. Finally, we were pronounced well again and returned to our respective billets. Pat and I had intended to keep in touch. Somehow, it didn't happen and we never met again. I was oppressed to be returning to Hornby Road, but now I was in another room and on my own. It had its advantages, privacy being one of them. Joyce told me that another girl had been moved into the bed I'd vacated that same day. 'The sheets weren't even changed!' she said. I hoped the poor girl hadn't picked up any of my 'flu bugs. Our landlady had been economising again.

This, if any, was the time to start my campaign of escape from Blackpool. I arranged to see the MO. It was surprisingly easy. Perhaps I'd been more ill than I realised. Whatever the reason, he saw my point and agreed that I should be returned to my former occupation. I was jubilant! I didn't mind that I'd have to wait for a posting now I knew that I'd be leaving. I still marched to Olympia each morning with Course 2IE, but no longer sat in the great hall. Now, I retired to a tiny office at the far end which I shared with a large, dark haired LAC, who was quite good-looking when his face was in repose. Unhappily, he had an agonising stutter and his features would contort in an effort to get out troublesome words. I had to bite back the urge to say the word he was desperately trying to eject – I felt very sorry for him.

In and out of the office from some as yet unexplored region came a young aircraftman, who clearly considered he was God's gift to women. I soon received his attentions. As though doing me a great favour, he said, 'Did anyone ever tell you what beautiful eyes you've got?', a self-satisfied smile spreading across his face. He was sure he must be the first. I was amused, but surveyed him coolly. '*Lots* of people have,' I said patronisingly. I could see my stuttering friend smiling approvingly in the background. In charge of the office was the stern faced warrant officer with the grey hair and rimless glasses who had put the fear of God into all of us. Now I found, at close quarters, a very different man. He was friendly and pleasant and not frightening at all. He was extremely amused when I confessed how terrified of him we all were. I soon found that if I was going anywhere in the evening and wanted to get away a little earlier, he would always let me go. He was an old softie at heart and quite approved of me, since I completed the various clerical tasks I was given in good time and I knew how to spell – nobody else seemed to! In this, at least, I had fallen on my feet for a while.

Rosemary, one of the girls in the billet, was engaged to a bomb-aimer in a PFF crew. She was desperately hoping to be posted to his station in 8 Group when she'd completed her course, and I knew she worked hard to this end. Towards the end of November, several days went by and no letter arrived for Rosemary. 'Don't worry,' I tried to comfort her, 'he's probably been operating nearly every night – you know what it can be like on Pathfinders – and he has just been too tired to write.' But anxiety was eating her up. She wasn't sleeping and it soon began to show.

A letter came, finally, but it wasn't from Bob. It was his flight commander who had written. It gave the news Rosemary had so dreaded, and gently said that little hope could be offered for his survival. She was devastated and in a state of almost total collapse. There was nothing we could do for her. Any of us would have held her and let her cry, and tried to give some feeling of comfort, but she didn't want to be held. She wanted to be left alone. Eventually she was taken to sick-bay to be sedated. Her grief touched us all. What became of her we never learned. She didn't return to the billet or the course, and we could only guess at her fate. Poor Rosemary. Once more it was *c'est la guerre*.

December – my birthday month – came in with clear, icy weather. Joyce suggested celebrating my birthday on our day off, which seemed a good idea. It was my 21st. I wasn't sure that I liked the thought of being 21 very much – I didn't seem to have been twenty years old for long enough. I quite liked being twenty. But the fact was inescapable. Twenty-one I was about to become, so it might as well be celebrated. Joyce took charge of the arrangements. Not that there was much to arrange – our meagre finances didn't run to it! A walk was a cheap enough way to spend the afternoon and we found our way to Stanley Park, stepping out briskly. In spite of pale sunshine it was bitterly cold. The ground was frozen hard and crusted with frost, and our breath condensed into a chilly mist. Our fingers were cold in our woollen gloves so we pushed our hands into greatcoat pockets for warmth.

The lake in the park was solid ice. We stopped to watch birds scrambling for scraps which bystanders had thrown on the surface. Ducks landed, spread feet skidding from under them, wings flailing, sliding along on their rumps. Swans shared the same fate, though more powerful wings saved some of their dignity. Gulls too, toppled and slid. We laughed at the spectacle, but with sympathy, knowing our own feet were just as liable to shoot from under us on the slippery paths. We were glad the birds were being fed – and decided it was time we were fed too. We found a teashop and had toast and jam, cake and tea. Afterwards, we went to see the latest Nelson Eddy – Jeanette MacDonald film. This, and the inevitable fish and chip supper later, was Joyce's birthday treat to me, and a generous one considering the prevailing shortage of ready cash. It was perhaps not the most wildly exciting of birthdays, but I quietly enjoyed it. There had been cards and gifts from home and a cake made by my mother, somehow contrived from her rations. It was delicious and I shared it with Joyce. And now here I was – a fully-fledged 21-year-old!

I'd wondered, in the days before, if I'd feel different – more grown up – but I didn't. Nothing had altered. It reminded me of the day, five years ago, when I was confirmed. Surely, I had then thought, there would be something rather miraculous, something glowing and splendid, after kneeling in church in my white dress and veil and being blessed by a bishop? I had tried to feel spiritual, waiting for what was going so wonderfully to change me. Nothing happened. I felt cheated when there was no glow, no splendour. Perhaps that was when belief fell away. Now I'd reached another high point. I was 21 – a special birthday – and I'd come of age. I was officially an adult and still nothing had happened. Were all the great occasions in life going to be like this? But I didn't brood for long.

A day or two later our squad marched smartly along a road in Blackpool, left right, left right, as a squad of airmen approached from the opposite direction. As it passed, a face came into focus. 'Jan!' I screamed. He saw me and, turning as he marched, yelled, 'Where are you?' '25 Hornby Road,' I shouted, sure he couldn't hear me and expecting our corporal to halt us and threaten me with a charge, but the street noises and clatter of marching feet had covered our voices. Jan had been a member of the concert party I'd also belonged to at Waddington. He was a dancer in civilian life and had taught me the dances we'd performed together at camp concerts. He was one of the 'gang', and seeing him made me suddenly and violently homesick for the days before Blackpool. I hoped we'd be able to meet and talk. I hadn't known that he had put in for a course of some sort, though I knew how unhappy he'd been as an equipment assistant. Seeing him was a great surprise. I told Joyce about it that evening as we prepared to go out. She sat in my bedroom, glad of the chance to get out of the pokey little room we had shared before my illness. Joyce was nice – an understanding sort of person, 12 years older than I. Thirty-three – *almost* middle-aged. A few grey hairs glinted in the waves of her thick fair hair. Her face was round and pleasant but a little crease was forming between her brows. Her eyes were blue and watchful.

Joyce had had her problems, including a romance which had ended in disaster. Plans for a wedding came to an abrupt halt when it was discovered that the bridegroom-to-be was already married. I understood about that. I'd had my own encounter with a married man. So we – Joyce and myself – had a number of things in common. She too had belonged to concert parties and choirs, and we both adored singing. We were missing the satisfaction and release it provided. Not singing – *really* singing – seemed a deprivation. Then we discovered the evening singsongs at the Tower. At first, we had been dismissive. 'Oh – *sing* songs!' But our need finally drove us there. We thus became part of a vast, assorted choir, singing old songs, popular songs, creating with our massed voices a great wave of sound. It rolled round the hall, rising, falling, reverberating, and crashing against the walls like the sea-waves outside. Reginald Dixon on the Mighty Wurlitzer organ provided a stirring accompaniment to a thousand or more voices. It was an emotional outpouring, given form by the words and music. If the words were trite and sentimental, the feelings aroused and released were real enough. Anxieties and unhappiness were in abeyance. We all just sang. Coming away at the end of it we felt light-headed and wonderfully free – and it was cheaper than alcohol.

I put in for Christmas leave. I hadn't spent a Christmas at home for two years, but now I longed more than anything to go. I don't think any of us would have been very welcome to stay on at Hornby Road in any case, nor would we have wanted to. I looked forward to it eagerly. The thought of returning to familiar, comfortable surroundings was immensely appealing. We had a pay parade. Now I could buy presents, after the interminable wait, standing at ease behind ranks of airmen and the Poles. We were always last to be paid. Presumably we were the least important. Or so we felt. But finally, cash in hand, we could go. The shops were packed with servicemen and women, all looking for that special gift for someone. I bought for my mother, my father, for Joyce and my friend Joan, and – what could I possibly send to Mike, overseas? In a department store, I ran into Jan again. We found a corner, where we were not jostled by the shoppers, and exchanged news. It was so good to talk to him. It transpired that he was also on a W/T course, and doing extremely well. He spoke enthusiastically of his own experiences and, after his former dreary job in Stores, I could appreciate his feelings even if I didn't share them. I told him I was off the course and would be going home for Christmas, and gave him what news I had of the other former members of the 'gang'. We parted, shaking hands and wishing each other a happy Christmas, and hurried off on our separate ways. It was the last we were to see of each other.

My leave arrived. Crammed in corridors, stumbling over kitbags and suitcases, seats all taken, sleeping soldiers, sailors and airmen, snores, sandwiches, cigarette smoke – it didn't matter – I'd be home eventually! And I was, to a loving welcome. Our Christmas was quiet, as all my home Christmases had been – there were no relatives to call in or visit. Lying in bed in the morning and being thoroughly spoilt by having my breakfast brought up to me was lovely!

There were presents and a tree and my mother always managed, somehow or other, to produce a cake and mince pies. For a few days the small family circle of my mother, my father and myself was all that I needed. I went to a dance at the Town Hall on Boxing Night and met an aircrew sergeant from Finmere, who was working in Flying Control whilst awaiting a posting. This gave us plenty to talk about as we danced. Other friends were there too and it was a pleasant enough evening, but I began to get the restless feeling that always set in after a few days of leave and felt rather shamefaced about it. Especially as I'd been so desperate to get away from the alternative.

As with all leaves, this one seemed at first to stretch ahead then suddenly contracted like a catapult and shot me back on to a train, waving farewell to my parents, taking me back to Blackpool. Changing trains at Crewe, I found an empty compartment. I leapt in and shut the door, hoping no one else would spot it – could I possibly be so lucky as to have the luxury of a compartment to myself, at least until the next station? No, I couldn't. The door opened and a khaki-clad figure got in. His shoulder flashes said 'Poland'. I pointedly looked away, keeping my gaze out of the window. I knew the Poles' reputation! This one was no different. He soon spoke to me – where was I going, what did I do, et cetera? I answered politely, but coolly. He was a rather charming young man, I had to admit to myself, but I wished he wouldn't keep moving closer. An arm crept round my shoulders. 'No!' I said firmly, pushing him away and moving to the opposite seat. 'Ah, please – you are so charmink!' he begged, following me. I moved away along the seat. He did too. I crossed over again. So did he. He tried to kiss me. I refused. Yet I couldn't be angry – it was a game. He was unabashed and smiling happily in the pursuit, even though rebuffed. Finally, he spread his hands and said, 'You are *vairy* nice girl – *vairy* good girl!' and desisted. After this, we talked. He spoke a little of Poland, of his family, of his friends in England with smiles, shrugs and expressive hands. I thought again of how much the Poles had suffered, and admired afresh their determination to survive and the unquenchable gaiety that seemed to be part of their nature. He shook my hand warmly when we parted. I wondered what his fate would be.

Blackpool again – and great news. A posting had come through for me! In nine days' time I was to report to a holding unit in Wilmslow to await further posting. Before then was New Year – and our billet had received an invitation from an aircrew billet in the next street to their New Year's party! Almost all of us went. It was terrific and we had a marvellous time. *Their* landlady was a dear. We danced, played games, ate, even drank a little, and two of the sergeants wanted to see me again. For a few days, I met them on alternate evenings – cinemas, dances, music hall – a whirl of gaiety for my last few days in Blackpool! It was great fun – until I got my appointments mixed and found I was seeing them both on the same evening! Neither was very pleased so I explained that I couldn't see them again, in any case, as I was posted. Then they both asked me to write. I did, for a while, but the correspondence gradually dried up as other interests and responsibilities came their way, and mine.

The day of my departure arrived. Goodbye, Blackpool! Even then I didn't get away quite unscathed. Another girl from the billet was also leaving – Olive, quiet and shy. With cases packed and kitbags sent in advance, goodbyes said, we were escorted to the door by our landlady. To our consternation, she became quite emotional and – horrors! – insisted on kissing us both, saying that out of the billet she had liked us best. She was very sorry to lose us! We did our best to smile under this unexpected onslaught, but it took us a little while to recover after we had escaped. Arriving at Wilmslow, we trudged up the hill to the camp. It was refreshing to see green fields and trees again and we rather enjoyed the walk, in spite of the grey, chilly day.

Olive and I spent eight days at Wilmslow, and it wasn't a very auspicious stay as far as I was concerned. Soon after arrival, I was on the carpet for sending my kitbag luggage in advance instead of keeping it with me as I should have done. My explanation of being unable to carry it was not accepted! I couldn't pretend that I was sorry though, thinking of the hill I would have had to drag it up. The small case I had brought was enough and carried everything I needed for a short stay. There was a good side though. I had to go down to the station every day to find out whether my kitbag had arrived, and I was pleased to have the excuse for leaving camp. How awful it must be, I thought, to be permanent staff at such a unit. Just numbers of girls arriving, never there long enough for any relationships to be made; unsettled girls, waiting only to move on. Girls with no intention of doing more than they needed to and with no incentive to do so, in the charge of staff who had to maintain discipline. It seemed to me to be a thankless, monotonous life with little to compensate. I would have loathed it and was immensely thankful that my job guaranteed a posting back to an airfield and flying. It was coming nearer and could happen any day.

My kitbag arrived and I got a lift back to camp with it. That achieved, I was allotted whatever jobs could be found. Those of us on disposal swept out the NAAFI, helped to cut up innumerable loaves of bread for tea in the cookhouse, or did any other odd job to keep us out of mischief. Time dragged. I made friends with another girl, Veronica, who was desperate to get away. She had been there a fortnight, she said. She was lean and quick and reminded me of a racehorse, well-bred, high-mettled and restless. She cared nothing for authority and seemed to do as she pleased. Often, in the day, we went to the empty NAAFI where a piano stood at the side of the stage. Veronica could play – classics, boogie woogie – anything. Boogie rolled off the keys with a lively, imperative rhythm and I couldn't keep still when she played it. Sometimes her choice fell on something classical, calm and serene – it depended on her own need at the time. Our private concerts were the best part of the day as far as I was concerned, and I was amazed that no one ever came to investigate.

My posting came through. So did Olive's. But still nothing for Veronica. I could imagine how she felt. She shrugged and wished me luck, but the desperate look was back. I fervently hoped she wouldn't be incarcerated much longer. I was destined for Upper Heyford. Not too far from home and, if not an operational station, at least an OTU. There would be aircraft again, and flying, and a broad green airfield to look out over! I was overjoyed. I almost didn't get away. Olive and I had collected our travel warrants from the Orderly Room the afternoon before our posting, as we had to leave camp at 7.30 am. Olive's train left at 8 am, mine at 8.30 am. At the Guard Room, we produced our travel warrants with a flourish for the SP's inspection. 'The last time we'll see you!' I thought. He examined them. 'You can't leave camp with these,' he pronounced. 'The Orderly Room stamp isn't on them!' He said it with some relish.

'But it *must* be!' we wailed. 'We have trains to catch – we're posted!' 'Sorry – you can't go till the Orderly Room has stamped them,' he repeated. It was just too much. I lost my temper. I treated the SP to my candid opinion of himself, his kind, of the inefficiency of the Orderly Room and a good deal more. I was almost crying with rage and frustration. Why I wasn't immediately put on a charge I don't know, but I wasn't. Either the SP was a sadist – or he may even have had a little pity in his make-up. Later, and calmer, I had to admit to myself that if he hadn't stopped us, other SPS examining our passes during the journey might well have done so.

We returned to the Orderly Room, waiting with frantic impatience for someone to turn up. Eventually a clerk appeared and we gabbled about the missing stamp. Our passes were examined, our postings checked, and at last our warrants were stamped. We flew back to the Guard Room. '*Now* can we go!' I demanded. He looked at the warrants and nodded. We were free!

Olive had by now missed her train, but prepared to wait at the station for the next one. She had no intention of returning to camp however many hours had to pass. We got a lift, and I was lucky – I just caught mine. I waved to Olive, and sank into a seat to relax after the fraught start to the day. I wanted to forget Wilmslow.

8

Life in Flying Control

Hours later, I arrived at the small country station which was my destination. It was late afternoon, and growing dark. At least I knew the ropes now and lost no time in telephoning RAF Upper Heyford for transport, which came in its own good time. From the back of the van, I breathed in the keen, clear air as we rattled along a narrow road which seemed to be arched over with tall leafless trees. I thought I could see stars through the high branches. Arrival at camp and the usual routine: reporting to the Guard Room, then the WAAF Guard Room, finding a billet and the drawing of bedding – and the meal, for which I was more than ready. I was impressed with the cookhouse – clean, pastel walls on which were painted at intervals, representations of fruit and vegetables and flowers. The food wasn't bad either. I went to bed early, and quickly fell asleep, wondering what life at Upper Heyford would be like.

Next day I officially 'arrived', reporting to the various sections and exploring the station. It was a peacetime station, and full of solid, permanent construction, with hedges and mature trees. A road divided the domestic part of the camp from the operational: the barrack blocks, mess-halls, WAAF site and Sergeants' Mess from SHQ and everything to do with flying. I went to Signals in SHQ, then walked up the roadway to Flying Control with an airman from Signals to escort me. Just behind the Watch Office, an Anson was parked on the tarmac. It was the first aircraft I'd seen on the ground since leaving Bardney, and I sniffed appreciatively the odours of fuel oil and dope. At that moment it was better than the rarest perfume to me, and it represented all that I had missed most in the preceding months.

Thanking the wireless op who had walked with me to the Watch Office, I went in and up to Flying Control. Inside, several people were busy at desks, but to one side, the man I took to be the SFCO – a squadron leader – was leaning negligently back in his chair and exchanging banter with an LACW. Another one with a tailored uniform, I noticed. As I approached she turned away, a short, squarish girl with green eyes and a freckled skin which, in the light, looked downy. Her red-gold hair was unashamedly on her collar. She had a generous smile, and bestowed one on me. The SFCO didn't. He observed me coldly, and spoke distantly. I disliked his sardonic expression and the scornful twist to his mouth. The drawling voice and sarcastic manner in which he spoke gave me the impression of a bitter and disappointed man. I did eventually find something in his favour, he was familiar with Waddington, and had modelled the Control Room as nearly as he could on Waddington's! His manner towards me became a few degrees less frosty when I told him I had worked there. Jacky, the girl I'd seen at first in Control, told me later, 'The way to get on with him is to stand up to him, don't let him bully you – he will if he can!' Forewarned was forearmed. I stood firm if I needed to, but I never felt comfortable or at ease with our squadron leader. There were other things to get used to. One was a 15-line telephone switchboard just inside the door, and the R/T operators were expected to operate this as well. It was an unknown quantity to me – I watched 'eyes' dropping and plugs pushed in and removed again, and switches moved back and forth, and wondered how I'd cope with this mysterious box of tricks. Like most things, it turned out to be not difficult at all and, after a little practice, it became automatic. So *that* was a relief.

Barbara, the corporal in charge, seemed pleasant enough and introduced me to the other girls, who all seemed disposed to be friendly. I was surprised to find a corporal R/T op – we hadn't had one at Waddo or Bardney when I left. There were two men R/T ops as well, one of them a corporal – an older man. Among the Control Officers was a Rhodesian flying officer. I chatted to him about 44 Squadron. He said it was his ambition to join it, or at least to be where it was. He also told me about Upper Heyford's gruesome nickname, 'the Rhodesian Graveyard'. Earlier, a Rhodesian course had suffered such heavy casualties that it had almost been wiped out before even getting to an operational station. The Hampdens they were flying were all written off – it had been a bad time for the station all round. Now Upper Heyford had Wellingtons.

A few weeks passed, and I began to feel that I was settling in, which I was keen to do. It wasn't happening as quickly as I'd expected though, and I supposed that my eagerness to get back to a proper station had led me to expect too much too soon. I'd been anticipating a return to the atmosphere and the companionship I'd experienced at Waddington and Bardney. But these were different circumstances and this, after all, was not an operational station. It didn't have the spirit of a station straining every nerve and every effort to the one objective: mounting a successful operation and a safe return, and living with the knowledge that some of the crews might *not* return.

But it wasn't unknown for a crew to go missing here. It shouldn't have happened but it did. Mostly through inexperience. Sometimes they turned up again, having landed at another station, found perhaps by a Darky call. At other times, they just disappeared and we never heard their fate. I heard the FCOs' surmise – maybe a navigational error, and they were lost in endless blackness over the sea, or did they encounter an enemy nuisance raider and get shot down unobserved? I remembered very well the Wellington that crashed and burned at Waddo, anything could happen and only sometimes would we know. But such things were not an everyday occurrence, for which we could be thankful. We rarely got to know any of the crews. They came and went as the courses rolled through. Circuits and bumps, night after night, then cross-countries, increasing in duration as the crews became more experienced. Then one day they would be gone, and the cycle started all over again. Crews came and went on an operational station too, but the squadrons were always there with the 'good shows' and 'shaky do's', and it was round the squadrons and their fortunes that the station revolved.

Still, here was the flying I'd longed to be involved with again and I knew well enough what the crews we trained were going to. They weren't yet the sort of men I'd encountered – but they would become so. I could only wish them luck. I began to feel a certain affection for the tubby Wimpies, and their pointing finger of a tail-fin, as I watched their take-offs and landings daily. There was always the odd entertaining incident, as when a pupil-pilot, on landing, selected 'undercarriage up' instead of 'flaps up' and gracefully sank to the deck, nicely blocking the runway intersection to the consternation of our FCO and the pilot's embarrassment. Two happy diversions occurred. A Lancaster landed one day, and the pilot reported to the Control room. I'd already noticed that the aircraft belonged to 9 Squadron – and the pilot was Charles, whose dicey operational take-off I'd once witnessed from Bardney's control tower. He came over. 'Pip! What are you doing here? I'd wondered where you had disappeared to! How are you getting on?' I asked for news of the squadron, and was glad to know Charles was still with it. He was a charming man in his quietly reserved fashion.

The second incident took place when a visiting Oxford came in and, as was required, the pilot came up to Control. This was none other than the Group Captain who had commanded RAF Waddington. Amazingly, he remembered me. He spoke to the Control officers, then came over to me. Smiling, he asked how I liked Upper Heyford. 'I prefer Waddington,' I replied. He smiled again. 'Yes, I can understand that,' he said. He wished me well, and departed. I had been amused to witness the expressions of surprise and disapproval on the faces of the two FCOs. A group captain, talking to a mere LACW! What next! As I was on duty, I was not required to get up and stand to attention so, of course, I didn't. Afterwards, I learned that he was in command at Silverstone, another OTU. I wondered if he missed Waddington too.

Flying Control brightened up when three pilots, all awaiting postings to further courses, came to us to fill in time and make themselves useful. Doug and Kit were sergeants, and Tony a pilot officer. Doug was quite the most handsome man I'd ever met. Six feet plus, tall, dark wavy hair, brown eyes, and features like a Greek god, yet he seemed totally unaware of his looks. There was none of the vanity or assurance that might have been expected; instead, he was pleasant and unassuming – even a little shy. He was, not surprisingly, engaged. I hoped he had a nice fiancée! Kit was nice, but a quiet man who kept himself to himself. Tony was 19, the youngest of the three, and a cheerful, open and light-hearted character. He was engaged too, to a girl in America. He had met her whilst training over there.

With their advent, social life improved. So far, I'd been invited by some of the other girls on outings – tea with Wanda in Oxford, a date with a couple of aircrew sergeants Barbara knew, both Canadians. They took us to a local pub and my partner for the evening, a W/Op AG known as 'Fish', bought me a pint of beer, taking it for granted that that was what I wanted to drink. It wasn't. I wasn't a beer-drinker. It seemed a tremendous amount of liquid – enough to drown in. It lasted me all evening. Perhaps that was the idea. I had also become friendly with Jane, my new room-mate. She was a sergeant-operations clerk, small, neat and extremely likeable. So was Betty, another ops clerk, a tall, slender girl with great charm. Both spent most of their time in Flying Control. I was beginning to know some very unusual and individualistic girls, mostly from Ops. Met and Signals, and to find their company very congenial. My early loneliness had dropped away. All the Duty Signallers, W/Op AGs screened after a tour of ops, were part of the good company I was finding too. I seemed to be integrating at last.

Of our three odd-bod aircrew, Tony seemed to be the one most often on duty when I was. We chatted occasionally, but there was plenty to keep me busy, even when no flying was in progress. In the morning there was always a bundle of Wilmots to enter – airfield serviceability signals from all over the British Isles and sometimes Iceland – and farther afield still. A good two hours' work. As well as test calls on the R/T, there was the switchboard to attend to. Towards mid-morning 92 Group rang up to be put through to the Station Commander, who then listened to the Group report. This usually started with a summary of Bomber Command's operations the night before and the results each group had achieved and, finally, went on to flying at the OTUs. I was eager to listen to 5 Group news if I could, for 44 and 9 Squadron results, and Tony, who hoped to be posted to 5 Group, was also keen to listen in. He was in particularly high spirits one morning. As we waited for the 5 Group news, he talked a stream of nonsense which had me in suppressed giggles. An outside phone rang, which the FCO answered. He put it down and fixed us with an angry glare. 'That, you may like to know, was the GC,' he announced. 'He says there's so much noise coming from the Control phone that he can't hear Group. In future, you two will *not* listen in.' We shrivelled. It hadn't occurred to us that we, too, were broadcasting. Why hadn't we thought to take the elementary precaution of covering the telephone mouthpiece! And now, no more 5 Group. We both felt very foolish.

Tony apologised to me, taking the blame for the incident, and invited me out to make up for it. I went – though I pointed out that it had been as much my fault as his. Anyway, I was older – by two whole years! I felt, if not exactly maternal, at least something like elder-sisterly towards him. He had a mop of fair hair and a youthful, pleasant face with boyish good looks, not yet touched by the strain of operations. That was still to come. Whilst we were out, he confided in me that he wasn't sure that he'd done the right thing in getting engaged. Who was I to give advice? 'Well, you are rather young to tie yourself down. If you have any real doubts, perhaps it would be better to break it off now – don't let it drag on too long.' I said. 'But I don't want to hurt her.' he replied. The age-old dilemma! I was engaged to Mike but having my own, very serious doubts. I felt I'd have to resolve them – and soon. My mother had not been happy about the engagement from the first. One reason, that Mike was a Catholic, another, because he was quite wealthy. In her own family experience, money had always brought trouble, quarrels and bitterness. She didn't want that for me.

As for my own feelings on these subjects – neither was of prime importance. Any religious pretensions I had were neutral. So far as I could see, each religion led to the ultimate end so why quarrel about it? And money – well, I'd never had a great deal but managed on what I had. More would have been nice, of course, but I didn't yearn for it. So my mother's doubts were not mine, but I had my own. Mainly that I didn't *feel* anything any more. I tried, when I wrote to Mike, to feel the emotions I had felt once – or had I?. Had I just imagined them because it seemed so romantic at the time? I had to admit I'd been attracted to other men since then. It seemed such a muddle, and I understood very well how Tony felt. I had only been 19 when I got engaged too. Well, I'd try to decide what to do – but I would put it off until I went home, where there were fewer distractions.

I could get home easily by catching a train to Banbury, and a bus from there to Buckingham. Or I could hitch – not too difficult. Occasionally, I met my mother in Banbury for an afternoon, when she had time and I was off duty, and we had tea together. She brought letters from Mike when there were any. He wasn't the most prolific of correspondents. One day, an airletter was opened. As she gave it to me she said, 'It just came open – I couldn't help seeing what was inside. He says something about it being you he wants to marry, not your parents. What does he mean by that? Doesn't he like us?' She was upset, but so was I. I couldn't remember what I'd written previously to cause Mike to make that remark – but she had read a part of *my* letter and I was offended. How did the letter come to be opened anyway? It wasn't the censor who had done that. I didn't really forgive my mother for some time. I asked Mike to write to me at Upper Heyford, promising to let him know in plenty of time if a posting was in the offing. I just wished my romances were less fraught. Now home wasn't the best place to think either, and still I put it off.

I had my bicycle back again and began to cycle round the lovely, lush lanes of Oxfordshire. It was late spring, and the trees and hedges were in fresh, green leaf. Hawthorn blossom smelled sweet and heavy along the roadside, and there were bluebells in the little wood on the corner of the road to Middleton Stoney. Not infrequently, a small group of those of us off duty cycled out together – Jane, Tony, Doug, perhaps Betty. We bowled merrily along, singing and whistling, once tra-la-ing Mozart's *Eine Kleine Nacht Musik,* which was very good to cycle to, or warbling popular songs as we spun through the countryside, carefree as birds. One of our favourite stops was at a little café at Weston-on-the-Green. Here, it was sometimes possible to have that extreme rarity, a real fried egg on toast! Or other such delicacies as pancakes with jam. It was a popular spot and we envied the airmen and women from the RAF camp just across the road from our café.

There was a nice little tearoom in Bicester called Mary's. It was rumoured that Mary's husband had been a fighter-pilot and was killed in the Battle of Britain. I don't know how true it was but we all gazed at Mary, a biggish, capable woman, with sympathy. In our eyes she had a sad, romantic aura. I had a 36-hour pass and thought I would go to Oxford. I had heard that a big dance was to be held at the Town Hall, in aid of one of the Service funds, and they were usually very good. Arriving in Oxford, I decided that something to eat was the first priority. Whilst eating in a snack bar opposite the New Theatre, three Americans came in and sat at my table. They were USAAF and quite crazy. Their actions and conversation were of the zaniest – but oh, so funny! I could scarcely eat for laughing. They included me among their company as though they'd known me for ages, and when we were all ready to leave they paid my bill, insisting that I should regard myself as their guest. They were catching a bus back to Wallingford and I was on my way to book in at the YW in Walton Street, so we were all heading in the same direction. I walked to Gloucester Green with my mad sergeants, sorry to part from such entertaining company. They invited me to come to Wallingford the following evening, but I was on duty then.

At the YW, I preened myself, ready to go to the dance. There I met a crowd of glider pilots, dashing in their maroon berets with light blue wings on Army battledress. The berets were, of course, tucked through shoulder-tabs. They were lively, energetic, and great fun. I stayed with them all evening, with a choice of partners for dancing. Each one was a good dancer and I didn't sit out a single dance. Afterwards, I slept like a log at the YW; the best night's sleep I'd had for ages. Next morning, I had a walk round Oxford, whilst waiting to catch the bus back to camp, and ran into three of last night's glider pilots. 'Come and have coffee!' they invited, and I did. We chatted amiably and I thought again what a good crowd they were. Then it was time to go our separate ways and we shook hands, waving gaily as we parted. It had been a good thirty-six.

It had been apparent, for some time, that preparations for a second front were under way. No one, of course, knew when but the feeling that it would be this year was strong. I longed to be where the action – or some of it – would be, and tried writing to R/T operators at 5 Group, 8 Group and 3 Group stations to see if anyone would be interested in an exchange posting. I must have written to fifteen or more stations, extolling the virtues of Upper Heyford – by now, I knew there *were* some – but the results were disappointing. One girl at a 3 Group station in East Anglia answered that she might be interested and would let me know in a week. I waited, hoping that something was going to come of it. She wrote, as she had promised, but she'd decided against it. One good thing came out of it though. I contacted Maureen again. We had lost touch after she was posted from Waddington, so I was very pleased to hear from her once more. She was now a corporal at Scampton and told me she had married a pilot from 57 Squadron – Steve – and he was now a staff-pilot at Barford St John, our satellite station!

I also heard from Pat, who'd been at Waddington and was now at Skellingthorpe. She too was a corporal and so was Vera, still at Waddo! It had all happened in late 1943, so I had missed out on the promotion stakes by my impulsive decision to try to remuster. Still, I remembered my early resolution, never to become an NCO! Clearly I wasn't going to break it. Pat described a bad night Skellingthorpe had experienced. Their aircraft had been recalled and told to jettison their bombs, but some returned with long-delay fused bombs still aboard. Whilst armourers were trying to get the bombs out of an aircraft, one of them blew up. The armourers were killed, and the windows of Flying Control blew out. Luckily for those inside there were then no casualties from flying glass. Anxiety was great in case the explosion set off a chain reaction in the other still-bombed-up aircraft but that, at least, didn't happen. It was a dreadful night for the station. Pat had been shocked and shaken, but stayed by the R/T. Some time later, she was awarded a Mention in Dispatches.

Joyce wrote, telling of fire and disaster, too. She was at Ford, a fighter station on the Sussex coast, and it wasn't unusual for bombers to come in there, short of fuel or in trouble. Getting up whilst barely light one morning, she heard a heavy aircraft coming in and looked out of the landing window in MQ, where she lived.

It looked towards the runway. What she saw was a Lancaster, coming in fast and obviously not going to make it. She watched, horrified, as it hit the runway, burst into flames and, bouncing up, cartwheeled off the runway and exploded. She was badly shaken by the sight and the thought of the crew inside. All of them perished. I thought it tragic that they should get back to this country only to become casualties here, but I knew it was all too common. Bomber Command's losses were not all over the Reich.

On a day off, Tony invited me to go into Oxford. 'How do you feel about taking a boat out on the river?' he enquired. 'Boating on the Cherwell,' I thought, oh yes! I agreed. I'd dress for it, too. It was a bright, sunny day and quite warm – I could take a summer dress and sandals – I'd risk it. I quickly changed in the Ladies' Room at Gloucester Green bus station and emerged in my blue and white gingham dress and sandals, having stuffed my uniform into a zip bag which I left at the bus station luggage counter.

Tony hired a boat and we pursued a leisurely course along the river, enjoying the special peace that rivers seem to have. We had bought some provisions on our way to the boatyard, and found a small island to moor beside. Here, we ate sandwiches and drank fizzy lemonade in the shade of the newly-leafed willows, their drooping, slender branches stirring gently in the light air. It was incredibly relaxing and altogether delightful. Oxford, I thought, was always delightful.

But time was passing, and we made a leisurely way back along the river. Hungry again, we looked for somewhere to eat. The 'Town and Gown', along The High, was as good as any. Eventually, replete, I looked at my watch and realised in horror that we'd have to hurry to catch the transport back to camp. So the peaceful afternoon ended with an uncomfortable rush. I dashed into the Left Luggage office at Gloucester Green and collected my bag, disappearing with it into one of the cubicles in the Ladies. I tore off my dress and the lights went out! Panic-stricken and in complete darkness, with visions of being locked in like the three old ladies, I opened the cubicle door and stepped out to see if I could find a light switch. The cubicle door, of course, clicked to behind me. My bag with my uniform inside; I, clad only in bra and panties, was outside. Really in a panic now, I felt my way to the door of the cloakroom and opened it. Not a sound, but there was a light in an office across the hall. 'Is anyone there?' I quavered. An elderly man emerged from the office, and I drew back rapidly behind the door as he came over. Poking my head round, I explained what had happened. 'Sorry, love,' he said, grinning. 'I didn't think anyone was in there when I switched off the lights. Hang on, I'll get you a key.' He limped over to the office and fetched it. 'Can you manage, duck?' he asked as he handed it to me. 'Oh, yes – yes, thanks,' I replied, hurriedly shutting the door on him. Once in the cubicle, I flung on my uniform feeling certain the bus would have gone without us. Outside, Tony waited and, seizing my hand, ran for the transport. Amazingly we were in time – just! When I told him what had happened, his hoot of laughter made a few heads turn. I could laugh too, then. I felt like something out of the *Daily Mirror*'s 'Jane' strip cartoon!

Early in June, postings came through for our three pilots. Tony was to go to 3 EFTS at Shellingford. Doug was going to train for Photographic Reconnaissance and Kit was also going to EFTS. Those of us who could, saw them off. We were all sorry to see them go. Flying Control was a duller place for their absence.

Coming off night duty a few days later, I was surprised to hear the radio in the WAAF Guardroom turned up to full volume. It sounded like marching music followed by an announcement in a foreign language, voluble and excited. Then, was it a national anthem and more announcements in different languages? What could it be I wondered for a moment, then realised – it must be D-Day! As I stood, listening, a thundering of engines filled the skies and waves of aircraft – Halifaxes and Dakotas – passed overhead, all towing gliders. Emotions surged up and I waved wildly, shouting, 'Good luck, boys! Good luck!' Tears came to my eyes, and I thought of the glider pilots I'd met such a short time ago – were they up there? How many of the men up there would see nightfall? There was no sleep that day – everyone who could listened to the radio for news of the invasion. This must surely be the turning point – it *had* to succeed. I chafed at not having been on duty on this momentous day.

We all listened to the news for days afterwards. There had

been terrible casualties on the invasion beaches, but we were there – and even advancing – we were going to make it!

Waiting on Oxford station, my mind elsewhere, I started as I became aware of someone standing in front of me. It was an aircrew sergeant, with a big smile on his face. 'Are you LACW Beck?' he asked. 'Yes' I hesitated, puzzled. 'You don't remember me, do you – Snowy Goodall from 44 – I used to go around with the Rhodesian boys!' 'Oh – of course I do!' Memory came flooding back and I could picture Snowy with his pale blond, almost white, hair – a thick thatch of it – and suntanned, creased features, New Zealand shoulder flashes on his uniform, in the midst of the Rhodesian crowd in the NAAFI or the cookhouse at Waddington. He continued, 'I was waiting to go into aircrew like most of them and now I've finally made it – I'm at OTU at Croughton. 'Whereabouts are you stationed?' When I told him Upper Heyford, he said, 'Maybe we'll see each other now and then, as it's not so far away?' Another grin creased his comfortable face when I agreed and gave him my address. It would be nice to exchange news with Snowy. My train arrived, and I waved to him as it pulled out.

Next day, I heard that I was to go to Barford St John. So were some of the other R/T ops and most of the Met assistants. Not a lot had been happening at Heyford for some weeks, but Barford was busy. I was pleased about the move. Smaller stations were usually friendlier and more easy-going, if Bardney was anything to go by. We were all rather looking forward to it. Transport was laid on to take us over – kit, bikes and all – which was fortunate as it was a day of heavy showers. Back to huts again, though these were of a better standard than Nissen huts. Still with the brute of an iron stove for heating – like every hut I'd seen. They were just a fact of service life. It was 'Salute the Soldier' week at Barford, and a dance was laid on at the Sergeants' Mess the night we arrived. Eileen from Met, Rita from Control and I all elected to go.

We had a marvellous time. An Australian F/O made a bee-line for me and, as we talked and danced, it emerged that he was a staff-pilot at Barford and had finished his tour with 467 Squadron at Waddington! I was so pleased to talk to someone who had flown from there – and he seemed nice, too. Medium height, dark hair, broad forehead and square shoulders – and a very entertaining sense of humour. When the dance ended, he asked to see me again. We went to a film in Banbury and we hoped to attend another dance in the Sergeants' Mess a couple of days later, but duty intervened and he was flying that night. Our next meeting had to wait.

I didn't lack company at Barford. I now came to know the Met girls much better than I had at Heyford, and I enjoyed their friendship. Jean, Welsh, small and quick, peering intelligently through large spectacles; Diana, who was dark and glamorous; Eileen, a doctor's daughter from Oxford; Mollie, the corporal, a little older than the rest – a pleasant woman; Pat, red-haired and rather shy. All became companions in off duty hours, as did a second Mollie, who was a clerk in Training Wing. I couldn't have met a nicer crowd of girls. Barford was living up to my expectations. I saw Snowy now and then; he had become a flight-sergeant. He invited me to go and meet his crew, and celebrate his 'crowns' in a pub at Fritwell. I spent a lively evening with them – a mixture of Australians and Englishmen, with Snowy from New Zealand.

I guessed he would enjoy coming home with me – the atmosphere of 'home' was something he'd missed. I surmised correctly. An easy going, obliging and generous man, he took to my mother and she to him. He went to see her and my father on his own, once or twice, taking rich fruit-cake sent from NZ to give to them. Sometimes I got a tin of it too. 'I'm sick of the stuff!' he said. I certainly wasn't, and I was very popular when I handed it around the hut.

I would have taken Colin home too – the Australian staff-pilot I met on my first evening at Barford – but it never seemed to work out. He was kept very busy with pupils, flying day and night. We managed some outings by day, though, spending warm afternoons at the open air baths in Banbury. We swam and splashed like children occasionally – just free and irresponsible for a brief time. Afterwards, we had tea at Wincott's or The Appletree tearooms and then it was back on duty for one or the other, or both, of us.

I asked Colin about his DFC, knowing I'd have to be very persuasive to get the story. At first he refused to say anything, so great was his distaste for a 'line', but eventually I got the story. The target was Hanover, the date 18th October 1943. He was stationed at Bottesford then. His aircraft was still over the target, having only just dropped its bombs, when a Ju 88 made three attacks on them. The pilot, Colin said, was evidently an old hand and concentrated his attacks on the mid-upper turret, just about blowing it apart. In the action, the unfortunate mid-upper gunner was hit in the eye and blinded. The rear gunner's guns had frozen up in the temperatures of 50 degrees below, and the Canadian gunner passed out through lack of oxygen; his hydraulics and oxygen supply had been cut off in the first of the night fighter's attacks. Colin's aircraft was now virtually defenceless.

As the fighter attacked again, he threw the Lancaster into violent manoeuvres, finally diving at 400 mph into the darkness. He said he expected the wings to break off at any moment! Things were bad enough though. In the fighter's last attack the flight engineer had been hit in the stomach, so now there were two wounded men aboard. Added to which both port engines were out of action, having caught fire. The fires were extinguished, but the engines could not be restarted and were now just so much dead weight. The control surfaces – aileron and rudder – were riddled by bullets and barely functioning. Colin couldn't hold the aircraft straight with his right leg on the rudder pedal, but the bomb-aimer was able to reach up from his position below and hang on to the pedal also, so some control, with great difficulty, was maintained. 'Thank Christ,' said Colin, 'the fighter lost us, and we didn't meet up with any more after that. It would have been the end of us if we had.' Colin next instructed the rest of the crew who were fit enough, to throw everything portable out of the aircraft – guns, bomb cannisters – everything that could go was jettisoned. 'Hopefully,' he said, 'to fall on some bloody German's head!' The weight loss enabled Colin to maintain a height of 6,000 feet. Their situation was still very dicey, but Colin was now determined to get home with his two wounded crewmen. He nursed his two good engines carefully as they roared on at full power, and prayed that they wouldn't seize up.

His determination paid off. They arrived at Coltishall, right on track, and tried to get down there. At first there was no response to the Very flares fired from the aircraft – the radio set, out of action anyway, had been jettisoned so they had no R/T. Colin circuited the airfield, firing more flares. Finally, someone noticed and the darkness of the landing ground was illuminated by the flarepath lights. The crew breathed a sigh of fervent relief. Colin came in, landing skilfully with his two engines, and as he touched down discovered that his starboard tyre had been hit and was as flat as a pancake. This caused a nasty groundloop – but at least they were down, and safe at last. The crew – he laughed, embarrassed – embraced him when they got out, grateful that he'd got them back to England. The injured men were taken to hospital where both survived. Colin rang Bottesford to let them know he was back, one and a half hours late. He had already been posted as missing. At last he retired, with the remainder of the crew, though not to bed. Their well-earned rest was taken on chairs in the Mess, with tables on which to rest their exhausted heads. I commented that it was a pretty poor welcome back after all they had gone through, and asked who was responsible for such miserable treatment. Colin shrugged. 'It's usual,' he said. At least he got a well-deserved 'gong'.

But who was to know just how much guts and bravery was represented by a ribbon and a piece of metal?

Colin also described to me the grandeur of the Alps by moonlight – though he said less of what waited beyond them and spoke, instead, of the stars on a clear night and how welcoming the constellation of Orion seemed on the return journey. I was fascinated by the depths of a starlit sky. I asked if there was any chance of going up in a Wimpy with him on such a night – a few circuits and bumps, perhaps? He promised to fix it if he could, but that didn't materialise either. When it might have been possible, it rained or he was too busy. On the really glorious, starry nights when he was flying I was, of course, on duty.

Flying Control at Barford was a reasonably happy place. The senior FCO, F/Lt Black, was inclined to be a little bossy, a little old-maidish, but underneath this, he was quite kind-hearted. F/Lt Bateson was an odd, unhappy man, good looking and in his 30s I guessed, but given to bouts of depression. He had pilot's wings. He was involved with Rose, our R/T corporal at Barford. An unlikely twosome on the face of it as she didn't seem his type at all, but it was obvious that she had great concern for him and perhaps that was all that mattered. Our Rhodesian, F/O Wilkie, was now at Barford, and F/O Dicker, a New Zealander, plus a recently commissioned P/O Rose, Rita, Wanda and I were the R/T complement and we were kept busy, often on three watches. We didn't have a switchboard to operate here, but we did make tannoy announcements, feeling a bit like a railway station announcer: 'The next train will be for Stafford and all stations to Crewe. ' Though our broadcasts were usually rather mundane: 'Will Sgt … report to the Gunnery Section', or perhaps something concerned with camp functions. I had mike-fright when I first spoke over the tannoy, in spite of all my R/T experience.

A new operator was posted to us, and great was my surprise to see yet another person whom I remembered from Waddington. She was from the early days, and had been a parachute packer when I first encountered her. It was Josie who had greeted Maureen and I on the day we arrived with the news that a fresh boy-friend was available every night! Now she had remustered as an R/T operator and here she was at Barford.

I wasn't especially pleased to see her, but we had a chat about the old days, and she told me that Lorna, the third of the trio to arrive at Waddington in 1941, was now a corporal at Wing, after being at Bottesford for some time. Josie's arrival eased our workload, but we now had another difficulty, shared with the girls from the Met Office. WAAF from each section were now detailed to take a turn at Site fatigues. We were expected to clean the ablutions and bath huts, the WAAF Naafi and the Recreation Hut, as there were now no general duty WAAF – the category had been abolished. Whilst realising the jobs had to be done, we didn't relish it. Our grumble was that we at the Watch Office were very small sections, therefore the unwelcome jobs came much more often to us as individuals than to the girls in larger sections like MT or the Orderly Room, and it seemed unfair. It was a sore point, and we tried using the Waafery Suggestion Book to air our grievance. Our complaint, however, was not kindly received by the WAAF officer. We were told we'd have to get on with it – which caused considerable indignation.

Barford's CO was posted to – where else? – Waddington! As he was engaged to our WAAF officer, he flew over to visit her from time to time – in a Lancaster, of course! His Lancaster, parked outside the Watch Office, drew me like a magnet, and when I came off duty, I climbed into it, revelling in the shape, the smell, and what seemed like the sweet familiarity of it. I couldn't claim to be so familiar – but it felt familiar, and I loved it. I clambered up to the pilot's seat and sat there, remembering my flight in another Lancaster with the Canadian pilot, Cliff Shnier.

Presently, some of the u/t aircrew sergeants climbed in. They were surprised to see me perched up there. I wasn't normally what they'd expect to see in the pilot's seat! I explained that I had been stationed with Lancaster squadrons before coming to 16 OTU, and told them I'd had a flight in one (omitting the detail of my airsickness). To my astonishment they began questioning me about the aircraft; what did the pilots think of them, were they good to fly? I answered as accurately as I could, and left before they got too technical. At least I could reassure them of the Lanc's popularity with the aircrew.

Colin had been posted on a four-week instructor's course to Lulsgate Bottom near Bristol a short time previously. I wrote and described my own bit of 'instructing'. His reply sizzled: '*You* actually had the confounded impudence to tell bods what it was like to *fly* in one !'Well, they *did* ask! During Colin's absence, the Met girls decided to give a party to celebrate various birthdays and anniversaries, and invited some of us from Flying Control to join them. We agreed with enthusiasm. A room with a piano was hired in a pub in Bloxham, the village just down the road from camp. All the staff-pilots were invited, and others whom we judged to be 'good types' – about a dozen in all, including the

Wingco who was now Barford's CO. As well as the pilots and a couple of navigators, two engineering officers, the Intelligence officer and our Rhodesian FCO were among our guests. One of them was Steve, Maureen's husband, a lively, likeable man. He was a pilot in A Flight and maintained friendly rivalry with Colin, who was in B Flight. They happily exchanged insults.

We had a wonderful time, singing, dancing, playing the fool. Our two engineering officers put on a very convincing duel, leaping on chairs and tables, feinting, lunging, weaving and dodging – until one was pinned to the wall with an imaginary rapier, coughing and choking. The 'rapier' was withdrawn, whereupon he sank to the ground dying picturesquely. They received a standing ovation. Drinks flowed, and there were sandwiches, and everyone was pleasantly happy. When the bar closed, the Wingco stationed himself behind the piano and produced his own supply of bottles, brought down from the Mess, and doled out drinks for us all. It was certainly true that Barford was a happy and a relaxed station! Of course, it was understood that no advantage would be taken of such off-duty fraternising whilst any of us were on duty – no one needed to make this clear, which was probably why it was such a success. The party broke up at midnight, and we returned to camp tired but elated. I wished Colin could have been there though.

But the month passed quickly, and he was back at Barford, having successfully completed his instructor's course. 'It was a bit late,' he said, 'as I've been instructing for six months already!' A new course came in, and the station was very busy. Colin was flying until 9 pm or later most evenings, and in Control we were back on three watches again. We now had to keep the aircraft times of landing and take-off, which, when circuits and bumps were the night's programme, kept us very busy. As well as logging them, we had to chalk them up on the Ops board, so were jumping up from the R/T each time the ACP rang through with a time. It seemed as though we had one ear to a telephone and the other to the R/T all night, logging conversation in one book and times in another, and more times on the board. Duty became a bit fraught.

It was at these times that we especially resented having to do WAAF Site fatigues. When on three watches, we should not have had to do them at all, but our WAAF officer seemed oblivious to our problem, and insisted. It was a pity Rose didn't feel able to go and explain the situation to her. Perhaps if she had made it clear that when on night duty we were actually awake all night, it might have made a difference. Or perhaps it wouldn't.

A parade was coming up in which the WAAF were to be represented. I organised a piece of self-preservation, not agreeing with parades. I paid a visit to the MO and told him that being on parade and having to stand to attention for any length of time made me feel faint, which was, well, going on for true! He, most obligingly, gave me a chit which excused me all parades and no questions asked! I was delighted with this, as our WAAF officer rather liked parades. Usually there was the legitimate excuse of being on duty, or sleeping after it, but this didn't cover every parade. Now, I was covered, and no one could argue.

We had a camp defence exercise early in August for one night. It commenced at 10 pm, and those of us not on duty were herded into the airmen's dining-hall, where we were to remain until 1 am. It was difficult, at this stage of the war, to see the necessity for it, but as usual ours was not to reason why! It was extremely boring, as nothing seemed to be happening, and for a while a group of us sat on the steps enjoying the balmy air and gorgeous moonlight. All flying had been cancelled for the exercise, and it was the best night for weeks. There were moans from other quarters besides ours. All we could do was swelter inside the hut, having been driven inside by an airman with a rifle and bayonet, who closed the doors behind us. Was he our brave defender?

Not having any idea what was going on was very frustrating, and knowing that I had an 8 am to midday and 4.30 pm to midnight shift the next day didn't improve matters. Eventually the hut's doors were opened and we were released – perhaps we had been designated 'prisoners' for the sake of the exercise? The truth was probably that we were required to be out of the way! Whatever the reason, a crowd of very cross WAAFs returned to huts and bed. The weather held and Di and I went into Banbury, where we went to the swimming baths. We had a luxurious sunbathe after our swim, then had a meal and went to the cinema, to see *A Canterbury Tale*. We voted it one of the best films we'd seen. It was a lovely day – the only sour note was Di's news from the Met Office that the weather was due to break. During the spell of sunny warm weather, some of the girls had taken to sunbathing behind our huts minus stockings, shirts and bras. The sun and the wind on bare skin felt wonderful, but it couldn't last. There was a spate of low-flying aircraft suddenly – we'd been spotted! That was the end of semi-nude sunbathing!

I walked on duty with Jean and Mollie, the Met corporal, and in spite of the earlier forecast, it was such a delightful evening that we chose to go the long way round, following the perimeter track. The green of the airfield stretched away almost as far as the eye could see, and the runways went on forever. The Watch Office seemed far away, on the peri-track curve. All was quiet, and we were in no hurry. Gazing upwards, I observed a band of delicately formed turreting cloudlets high and remote in the imperceptably deepening blue. 'What are those clouds called?' I asked. Mollie told me, 'That is alto-cumulus castellanus.' What a lovely name, I thought, repeating it to myself and finding pleasure in the rhythm of the syllables, whilst my eyes took in the faraway loveliness of the cloud formation. Alto-cumulus castellanus. Less lovely was something else seen in the skies this time at night. Several times after flying had finished for the night and everyone had gone, I stood at the Control room window looking at the stars. Towards the south-east, I had seen an orange streak, far away, rising rapidly into the sky. Puzzled, I mentioned it to F/Lt Black one morning. He told me that what I had seen was probably a V2. 'But would it have been visible as far inland as this?' I enquired doubtfully. He assured me that it would. What an eerie, unpleasant feeling it gave me the next time I witnessed that soaring, malevolent streak of light. In moments it would reach the apex of its climb then fall, bringing death and destruction with it, and I could only stand and watch.

September drew on, with cold mornings and evenings but lovely still afternoons of sunlight and blue skies. Mollie, Di and I went for a walk. It wasn't an afternoon to waste. We meandered along country lanes, spellbound by the mellow gold of the autumn sun, and we found blackberries in the hedges. Elderberries hung in dark, shining clusters and wild rose hips glowed red. Michaelmas daisies and early chrysanthemums bloomed in the gardens we passed, as well as late roses. We came to Milcombe, a village about two miles from Barford. On the outskirts was a thatched cottage, picturesque as a cottage should be, with a most enticing orchard beside it. The trees were heavy with rosy-red apples and purple plums which we longed to sample. We went to the door and knocked, intending to see if we could buy some. An elderly man answered and, on hearing our request, invited us through into the orchard, where he filled two paper bags with apples and plucked a basketful of plums and gave them to us! This generous man would accept no money from us and furthermore told us to come back for more whenever we liked.

The scent of the ripe fruit was intensified by the warmth of the sun as we carried our loot back, sampling it along the way. What a perfect afternoon this had been. The plums were sweet and juicy and we got through rather a lot, but there was still enough, with the apples, to share round Hut 3 when we reached camp and I kept some back for Colin. He had, after all, only yesterday given me more chocolate and another tin of orange juice saying: 'Of course, it's a ginormous sacrifice – but I think your need is greater than mine!' This because I had a cold, and he thought the vitamin C might help.

In fact, I was being rather well looked after. Coming off duty at midnight with the Duty Signaller, we went in to supper together. Being aircrew, he got a fried egg with his chips. I watched enviously as I'd been given cold meat. But a generous heart was beating beneath his brevet. He insisted that I took the egg – it was good for me! The concern for my health continued. I happened to take in a cup of tea for another duty signaller next day, and he said, 'Ah! I've been waiting for you – I think you should have this!' 'This' was an orange – something very rarely seen, but there had been a recent issue to aircrew. I said I really couldn't take it – but the answer was again that it would do me more good that it would do him. I was very touched at all this generosity. Then came another cake from Snowy – a 4 lb bumper issue! Hut 3 loved New Zealand cake.

Colin had a 'shaky do' on a flying detail one night. In a Wimpy with a pupil-pilot at the controls, the port engine cut at barely 20 feet. Colin, knowing he had only seconds to save the aircraft and all in it, acted. The Wimpy was one of a very few at Barford which had dual controls, and he took over. He was unable to retract the undercarriage because it could only be operated from the port motor. Take-off flap was still on and the aircraft was nose up and starting to climb, whilst still on a low airspeed – a fatal combination. Somehow he wrestled the aircraft up, using the starboard motor at continuous full power, and managed to come round and land half expecting the engine to blow up at any moment. It was a shaken and relieved crew who descended from the aircraft, none more than Colin, who recognised more clearly than the inexperienced crew how close they had been to death. He received a letter from the Group Captain commanding 16 OTU, commending his first class effort in getting the aircraft safely down under the circumstances. 'I think it is one of the best shows I have seen for a long time,' he wrote, 'and feel you are entitled to the greatest credit. I am recommending a green endorsement in your log book.' I didn't know whether to be glad or sorry, that I hadn't been on duty that night. I knew it had been a nerve-wracking experience for Colin, but operational flying bred fast reactions and, thankfully, they hadn't failed him.

Instructing was no sinecure – Colin also had an engine failure on a Wimpy at 1,500 feet, but said that there was no problem in comparison to the one just after take-off. He described another unpleasant experience. It was an exercise instructors were expected to demonstrate to pupils – a landing without flaps. 'I did it once – but never again on a Wellington! I had to come in at treetop height some five miles from the runway, touching down at the very beginning of it at around 100 mph. The damn thing took a hell of a long time to slow down sufficiently for me to apply the brakes without tipping the aircraft on its nose. We only finally came to a stop just as we were running out of runway. This exercise could only be attempted when a wind of some 15–20 mph was blowing. I wouldn't try it again – too dangerous!' Colin didn't like our old Wellingtons. In his experience, he said, they had too many vicious characteristics and were not well maintained either. He preferred Whitleys on which he'd done his own operational training and found much gentler to fly. Instructing was supposed to be a rest. Some rest, I thought!

It wasn't long after this that Colin's repatriation came through, and the next day he was gone. We scarcely had time to say goodbye. It was very sudden. Colin left England's mists and rain for the sunshine of his own country – and I was sorry to see him go. I knew I'd miss his company. But Johnnie was coming back. I'd had one letter from him back in March, whilst he was in Switzerland, then silence. Now he'd be here any day. His letter said he would be in England only a short time before being repatriated to Canada, but he wanted to come to Banbury to see me. I looked forward eagerly to seeing him again and to hearing all that had happened in the last 14 months. I still remembered vividly the sudden foreboding I'd experienced when I last saw him just before take-off. Then I could only sit and watch as his aircraft sped along the runway on an operation I knew it wouldn't complete, but that was all over now.

The day arrived for his visit, and I met his train at Banbury station. I watched the descending passengers and thought I saw him – then suddenly he was at the ticket barrier, smiling as he came through and forgetting to hand in his ticket. The collector had to remind him. He took my hands and, for a moment, we didn't know what to say. I saw that he was a Warrant Officer now. The park seemed the best place to go and we made our way there. We sat on a seat in the autumn sunshine. I was glad the sun shone for our meeting. Once more there was silence and smiles, but then the flood-gates opened and we talked and talked. Johnnie told me his story – how the aircraft came down in Italy, and the crew split up hoping to avoid capture. Sadly, Eddie, the flight engineer, was killed in the crash. After some time on the run, Johnnie was caught by the Germans and put into a prison camp. He believed that at least some of the rest of his crew were also taken prisoner but had no contact with them.

Never one to give in to circumstances Johnnie planned an

escape and was back on the run again within a short time. He didn't tell me all that happened between then and getting to Switzerland but it couldn't have been easy. In Switzerland, he was interned with other allied airmen. It was by no means a hard life there. In Davos, they were housed in a gasthof and given suitable clothing. They could go skiing and could do almost what they liked, except leave the country. In peacetime it would have been almost a rest cure, but this was war and the time came when Johnnie could no longer stand the easy life. Again he made his escape, this time into France, where he met up with a Resistance group and worked with them. Finally, threading his way through the German lines, he found himself close to a forward American unit. Knowing what was in front of them he lost no time in making contact. He was interviewed by an incredulous American general whose first words were, 'And what's a skinny little bastard like you doing in this neck of the woods?' Having been on very short rations for some time Johnnie appreciated this friendly welcome! However, after he had convinced the general that he was who he said he was and passed on his valuable information, he was given a good meal – the first for some little while and was soon on the first leg of his journey back to England. To Marseilles, then by boat to a Middle Eastern port and from there, he was flown back. There must have been so much more detail – but there wasn't time to tell all of it. Anyway, he'd promised that there'd be no 'line-shoot' when he saw me!

Later we discovered that it was almost evening so went to look for refreshment. We found it in Mrs Brown's Cakeshop where the original Banbury cakes came from and, in the low-beamed tearoom with a table in the big inglenook, we enjoyed a meal, and afterwards went for a drink to celebrate meeting again after all that had happened. We arranged to meet again the following day when I was off duty for the afternoon. We planned a late lunch and a visit to the cinema, and Mrs Brown's for tea again. Earlier, to make sure of no last minute panics, it seemed sensible to book a taxi to take me back to camp. I was on duty at 4.30 pm. We went into the local office to arrange the time and place for the cab to pick me up. 'What name?' said the clerk. 'Warrant Officer Merchant,' Johnnie replied. The clerk asked him to repeat it, which Johnnie did, but he still didn't get it. Johnnie tried again. 'Merchant,' he said distinctly, 'as in Navy.' The clerk got it. He wrote, 'Warrant Officer Merchant-Navy'. Our eyes met and, almost convulsed, we ran out before our giggles overwhelmed us. Outside, we spluttered and chortled with held-back mirth. 'Ah! Warrant Officer Merchant-Navy I presume!' I exclaimed when we next met. It became a catchphrase. But I knew Johnnie wouldn't be around for long and as he was stationed near Manchester, his visits to Banbury were limited. In what seemed like no time at all, he had to tell me there would be no more visits. At the station, I saw him off for the last time, sad and regretful. It was war and there had to be partings – I was already very familiar with that, but they didn't get any easier. I also knew there was the girl back home.

I received a summons to our WAAF CO's office. 'What now?' I thought. But it was to tell me an appointment had been made for me to go to Air Ministry for an interview for a commission. I had completely forgotten that Joan and I had put our names on a list to be considered for one early in 1943, just before we had moved to Bardney. It wasn't that I'd had any great desire for a commission; it was at a time when we had both thought the conditions in the Officers' Mess would be preferable to the ones we had. I had fancied being a Code and Cypher officer, and I remembered James's urging on the subject. Time passed, and it began to seem so long ago that I was convinced I'd hear no more about it. Now, I prepared for the interview and went to London on the appointed day, presenting myself to the Board along with several other candidates. I found the interview not too terrifying – in fact everyone was very pleasant. But I was told there were now no vacancies for Code and Cypher officers – would I be prepared to consider WAAF 'G' officer? That meant working in a WAAF Section – admin, discipline. 'No,' I said. And that, of course, was that. I had no regrets.

Shades of Blackpool – as autumn progressed, I had a non-stop series of heavy colds and coughs. I still coughed, and night duties crammed with circuits and bumps were a misery. Cigarette smoke irritated my throat, and continuous talking on the R/T aggravated my coughing. I went home on a thirty-six hour pass and saw my own doctor. As I guessed he would, he confined me to bed and wouldn't let me return to camp until I'd improved. The next time I had bronchitis I was sent to the Horton Hospital in Banbury for a chest X-ray. But it was clear so it was back to the mist. There were many American troops camped around the Banbury area and it was inevitable that most of us came into contact with them at some time, whether we wished to or not. When I did, it always seemed to be when I was in Mollie's company. This was Mollie from Training Wing. She was engaged and her fiancé was a POW, to whom she was utterly faithful. She was the last person to seek out American – or any other – male company. She was a sensible, reliable girl with lots of humour and character. She and I hitched back from Banbury one evening. A jeep stopped for us. There were already two soldiers in the back seat, and they moved up for us to squeeze in. The driver was obviously from the Deep South, and we listened in fascination to his accent – just like the movies!

Rather to our dismay, a bottle of cider was produced and passed around as we drummed along. Mollie and I had to partake – there was to be no argument. Furtively wiping the bottleneck, I tipped it to my lips, and not being adept at drinking from a bottle I got rather more than I'd intended and nearly choked. Mollie, taking note, tipped it not quite far enough and avoided drinking any. The driver, it seemed, had quaffed fairly deeply. Feeling very devil-may-care, he announced, 'A'hm gonna drive you all up that bank – hold tight!' and flung the jeep head-on at the steep grassy bank topped by a hedge, which bordered the road. Mollie and I clung together and hoped for the best. 'OK – now we'll come down again!' sang our driver and backed rapidly down the road, where he put his foot hard down on the accelerator. 'Please – would you mind *not* doing that again!' I said in my best 'commanding officer'-type voice, when he slowed as another steep bank beside the road came in view. He gave me a surprised glance and said, 'OK,' and we shot forward again. Bloxham was reached in double-quick time, and we were set down all in one piece – if shaky – and very relieved. No more American lifts, we vowed.

I arranged to meet Mollie in Banbury again a few days later. At Adderbury, a tall young American soldier got into my compartment. After a short while he spoke to me asking if I knew the times of the trains back that evening. I told him and the conversation continued on more general lines. As we approached Banbury, I told him I was meeting a friend at the station. The train drew in, and I saw Mollie, also talking to an American as they stood on the platform! Bob – he had told me his name – got out with me. Mollie and I looked at each other, and burst into laughter. What could one do about these Americans? Mollie's American left, but mine didn't. I intimated that we were going to the pictures. 'Then let me take you both!' he pleaded. We weakly gave in. He was so pleasant, so eager to please that it would have seemed churlish to refuse.

After the film he took us to a café for a snack. We all caught the same train then and when he didn't alight at Adderbury, I asked why. 'I'm going to see you back to camp,' he said. 'Oh – that's very kind of you, but we'll be all right – and how will you get back to Adderbury?' I asked, concerned. 'Why, walk!' he laughed. We were touched by this piece of gallantry, unnecessary though it was. He had told me he'd be going to France very soon and wanted to see me again. I had no intention of starting an American romance but he was such a genuinely nice boy and seemed very young. Later, I learned that he was 20. I invited him home on a day off, and he was so pleased. He hadn't been in an English home before and was touchingly appreciative. My mother made this big American very welcome. He was careful and gentle, as very large men are, in order not to damage the hand they shake or the chair they sit on.

What my father thought of the procession of men from overseas who turned up at 14a Market Square I never knew. He said very little, leaving the socialising to my mother, knowing she enjoyed it as she enjoyed mothering those who seemed to need it. Bob asked me to write to his mother and, of course, I did. From Johnnie's mother, I'd learned how much news of a son meant in wartime. For the same reason, I corresponded with the wife of an Australian soldier – an older man – whom I met on the train to Buckingham one day. I didn't see her husband again, but the letters to and from his wife continued. Bob went to France with his unit – the 424th Infantry Regiment. His mother sent me a cutting from the local paper, which described the action they were in – the Battle of the Bulge in the Ardennes. From the hard fighting, Bob emerged safely and had been promoted to sergeant. After this, came a frontal assault on the emplacements of the 26th German Division in the Siegfried Line. The Combat Report afterwards said that the German Division ceased to exist as a combat unit after the attack – so what dreadful things he saw at this time I shuddered to think. But he came through it all unscathed, at least physically, and returned to the US with his unit directly from France. I didn't see him again, though I still wrote to his mother – this was another continuing correspondence, and I enjoyed it.

Bob had wanted me to be 'his girl', but though I liked him and felt affection for him, I couldn't cope with more. I didn't want any deep involvement for a while. I tried to explain this to his mother since he had told her how he felt – and I hoped she could understand. Bob too, for that matter. Perhaps she did, as she kept on writing. Maybe she was even a little relieved! I knew Bob would find another girl – and eventually he did. His mother told me, very thrilled about it all. I was happy too. I could stop feeling slightly guilty. At last.

9

Arrival of the Flying Fortresses

The next Americans to come my way arrived in Flying Fortresses! Forty nine of them. They were diverted to Barford on their way back from a daylight op because their base at Podington in Northants was closed in by bad weather. It was an incredible sight as one after another the B17s came in. I thought they were never going to stop. Eventually, they were dispersed all round the airfield. Barford had never seen so many aircraft all at once. The crews began to make their way to the Watch Office. I was making tea, so started giving cups of tea to the Americans as they came up feeling that they must need it. But soon I ran out of tea and could do no more. The Met girls from downstairs produced another supply but that was rapidly exhausted. There were Americans crowding out Control, in the Met Office, sitting wearily on the stairs, and sitting outside. Men in leather flying jackets and boots, hung about with flying-gear. There were nearly 500 men – how was Barford going to cope? The Met girls and I came off duty. As the first crew to whom I'd dished out tea was still in the Watch Office, I asked the pilot if we could go and look at their aircraft. It was the nearest one to the Watch Office. Several of them said they'd be happy to show us around, and we went to look at, and in, it. It was named after a popular song of the thirties – 'I'll get by' – 'as long as I have you,' the next line continued, and as long as the wings of the B17 bore them so they did. Jean and I were fascinated to see the interior, which was quite differently laid out to that of a Lancaster. We were given handfuls of candies and gum – each of the crew gave us the remainder of their candy rations, and pockets and hands were filled. Another of the crew – the tall navigator – took out a Met Report card, and got the rest crew to autograph it. He wrote, 'A swell bunch of people, you English – thanks for everything. H. A. Gray, Navigator.' The pilot's signature was Dom Taurone.

As we came away from the aircraft, one of the crew who had been with us said I had reminded him of an occasion soon after they came to England. They were stationed at an airfield, not yet operational. Early one morning, when the station was just stirring a Lancaster made an emergency landing. The news went round like wildfire and men poured out to watch, greatcoats thrown on over pyjamas – everyone curious to see the bomber they'd heard so much about. It was plain that the aircraft was badly damaged. Two engines only were functioning, and the rear turret was shot to pieces. The fuselage was full of holes.

The noisy excitement among the spectators died down and there was a hush as the Lancaster rolled to a standstill. An ambulance and the fire tender were waiting. The latter wasn't needed but the ambulance was. The crew came out – those who could. The pilot said, 'My navigator's wounded. Both gunners are dead.' The American doctor and his orderlies hurried into the aircraft and gently lifted out the wounded man and put him into the ambulance. They went back for the bodies of the gunners. Only one was brought out. The rear-gunner had been obliterated. The orderlies emerged looking green and shaken. Others looked in, but hastily withdrew. The rear of the aircraft was not a pleasant sight, and for most it was the first glimpse of violent death. Someone said, awed and horrified, 'Is it always like this?' 'It sometimes is,' said the pilot wearily as he climbed into a waiting jeep.

Next day trucks with their own ground crew arrived, and they swarmed around the B17s, getting them ready for departure. Later, the aircrews were driven out to their aircraft and soon, one by one, they lined up to take off. This was another enthralling spectacle as the first big aircraft became airborne, then the next, and the next, and the next, until all 49 were airborne. When they had all departed, the groundcrews left and the station, from heaving and buzzing with activity and noise, was strangely quiet. In fact, everything was rather flat after our American invasion. But something interesting was always just around the corner.

I had nine days leave. It was the first I had had for ages, as leave, except for 36-hour passes after night duty, had been cancelled for some time before D-Day and after. There was a backlog to make up, but my turn had finally come round. I went to Lincoln for a few days and, whilst in this lovely city, I ran into several people I'd known at Waddington. Even if I hadn't known them well it was good to hear news and gossip from the station. During such a casual meeting, I heard a strange story from Ivy, a parachute packer. In a snack-bar over tea, she told me how once, at Lindholme (her previous station) she and Madge, her companion, had been waiting to collect parachutes from the crew of the last aircraft due back. The wait had been a long one.

They were tired and chatting idly. Then both stopped, listening when they heard the heavy tread of flying boots on concrete, approaching. 'Oh good – they're back,' said Ivy. 'Funny – I don't remember hearing the Lancaster land, do you?'

The footsteps reached the door of the section and stopped, but no one entered.

'Oh – they're playing about!' laughed Madge. Both ran to the inner door, Ivy flinging it open. Madge opened the main door. No one to be seen. The girls called, but there was no response.

'Well – are they back or aren't they? What on earth's going on?' Ivy exclaimed. They looked at each other, not knowing what to think. A message was brought to them later; they could go off duty. The aircraft was confirmed as lost. And the message was timed at *exactly* the time the girls had heard the footsteps.

Ivy and Madge gazed at each other aghast. So *what* had they heard? They shut the doors and fled back to their billet, hoping that sleep would help to dispel the chill and shock they felt.

'I never believed in ghosts until then!' said Ivy. I believed her. It made me feel cold too.

When I returned home there was a card from James. I'd told him in my last letter that I was coming home on leave, and now he asked me to send a wire to let him know if I could get to York, even if only for 36 hours. He would get a pass and meet me there. That, I thought, would be lovely. Although we had written since he left Waddington, I hadn't seen him since then. He had been stationed so far away, first Wigtown, in Scotland, then Bridlington. When he had leave, he had naturally gone home to Birmingham to see his fiancée. I left for York, arriving just after 6 pm. James hadn't yet appeared, but the arrangement was to wait in the Station Hotel lounge. It wasn't long before James' tall figure appeared through the door. It was the first time I'd seen him in his officer's uniform, and I thought he looked impressive. The pipe was still the same though. He gave me a hug, and I enquired if I should salute him? 'LACW Beck, are you asking for trouble already?' he said sternly. 'Watch it, or I'll have you on a charge!'

We had a drink, and went to look for somewhere to stay. Fortunately, the George Hotel found us rooms. York seemed pretty full up so we were lucky. It crossed my mind to wonder what some of the girls would think if they knew that here was I, spending the night in the same hotel as the RAF officer I'd come to meet! Undoubtedly, they would think the worst. But they would have been wrong. There was great regard between us – no more.

The following day, we wandered around York. I was enchanted with it – the City walls and Clifford's Tower, the mediaeval buildings and, most of all, the Minster. In the Minster that afternoon was a concert which included Mendelssohn's *O For the Wings of a Dove*. Of course, we went. As ex-members of Waddington's choral society, we wouldn't have missed it. The Rose Window glowed and the interior of the Minster was full of grace – and the choir was magnificent. It was all so beautiful and so satisfying. We came away feeling blessed. There was so much to see in the city, and I loved it. The time whistled by, inevitably, and James was wonderful company, so that when the time came for him to leave the next morning, I couldn't help but feel sad. James had been a staunch presence in my life since Waddo days, even if a background one; I didn't know if I'd see him again now that he was getting married. He told me of his plans the evening before. He also said that this didn't prevent him from being my friend – but I wasn't sure. I thought it probably would, and reflected that if I were his wife I might think that it *should*.

I hitched back to camp. This time, a Canadian in a radar van picked me up. North America seemed to breed mad drivers! Corners were taken on what felt like two wheels, with very little regard for any other traffic on the road. The cylinder-cap was missing from the bonnet and a spray of muddy water spattered the windscreen. Eventually the water stopped and steam began to rise, and I fully expected the whole thing to blow up as we rattled along. I voiced my anxiety. 'Oh, that'll be OK,' he said carelessly. 'We're nearly there now.' He was delivering the van to Hinton-in-the-Hedges. 'And anyway – *I* shan't be driving it again!' I got out, and he swung round into the lane leading to the camp. Hard luck on whoever *would* be driving the van again, I thought.

I was completely broke after my leave, but payday came in time for me to join Mollie and Di for an afternoon in Banbury – a rather special one. Moiseiwitch was giving a piano recital in the Town Hall, the proceeds of which were going to the Merchant Navy Comforts Fund. It was gorgeous. Bach, Beethoven, Chopin, and some of Debussy's lovely studies – Jardins sous la Pluie, La Fille aux Cheveux de Lin, some Granada, and Brahms' Variations on a Theme of Paganini. Everyone clapped madly and the old man bowed sedately, his mane of grey hair falling forward. I doubt if Banbury Town Hall had heard anything like it before.

It was 1945 and, like everyone else, I began to wonder about demobilisation. I had by then been posted back to Upper Heyford. The war seemed as good as won, though there was plenty of bitter fighting still going on. There was no doubt about the outcome now – it was just a matter of time. The spirit of urgency had gone, for us at least, and work was just routine, lacking the interest and excitement it once had. Admittedly Mosquitos had recently replaced our Wellingtons, and we enjoyed operations with these fast and graceful aircraft. Barford had its share of them too, and we were shocked one day to hear a WAAF had been taken up in one – unofficially of course – and it had crashed, killing her and the pilot. A few days after this sad news, an airman whom I didn't know at all stopped in front of me as I walked to the Mess. He exclaimed, 'Oh – I *am* glad to see you – I thought it was you who'd been killed in that Mossie!' I was quite touched, and pleased that he was pleased – but I never did find out who he was.

Elsa was now an invaluable companion. Together, we listened to classical concerts on the radio. So many orchestras were available to us! The London 'Phil', the London Symphony, the Scottish Symphony, and more. Light orchestras too – there was music in plenty. Occasionally I accompanied Elsa to her book-lined flat in Oxford, where a gramophone and a stack of classical records gave us hours of pleasure. Also, I met many odd, charming and different people at her flat – people of many nationalities, and all part of the hotch-potch of wartime Oxford life. Arriving back from leave I found I was down for a day's Jankers' before going back on duty. I was rather put out. This was a scheme for getting extra duties done and everyone in the ranks took a share in it from time to time when returning from leave. 'Nice welcome back!' most of us thought sourly. My share was peeling mounds of carrots and onions in the cookhouse. I could understand the cooks passing on *this* job, I thought as I mopped streaming, stinging eyes.

Then Leo came into my life. He was a wireless operator/mechanic who often joined Elsa and me in the cookhouse or the NAAFI, and sometimes came into Oxford with us to a concert. Elsa and Leo both worked in SHQ Signals and, having similar interests, knew each other well. At that moment, I wasn't very interested in Leo's feelings. I wanted just to be quiet. His attentions, undemanding as they were, irritated me. Peace – it was peace that I wanted. Sometimes coming off duty alone at night, I looked up into the cloudy dark, willing the wind to carry me high into the black emptiness; half-afraid of the desolation and the absence of all human warmth I'd find, and half-welcoming it. Almost I thought I could let go – but, of course, I couldn't. Coming into my room and getting into bed was suddenly all that I wanted after all. The phase passed.

As was inevitable I slowly came to accept Leo, and to like him. A tall, dark, serious young man. At only 21, he was younger than most I had known yet he seemed older than his years – I had imagined him to be about 25. He was wise and knowledgeable about so many things and there was an inner loneliness too, which found an echo in me. Leo loved music, and seemed to know the classics intimately. Living in London, he told me he'd started attending the Proms at the age of 12 – on his own!

I met most of the wireless ops and mechs from SHQ, and the Flights through Leo. Tall, cadaverous-looking Bill, a good friend of Leo's, who was an artist. John, a small Irishman, 40-ish, handsome, with the temperament of an actor; he loved the stage, and should indeed have been an actor instead of the teacher he was in civilian life. Derek, with his background of public school and Cambridge, quite happy as an 'erk'; a most attractive and entertaining man. Friends grew around us. Tosci, a corporal we came to know well by sight because he seemed to appear wherever we were – at CEMA concerts on the camp, or gramophone recitals – even when we were just sitting in the NAAFI he appeared as Duty Corporal, putting up the blackouts. Finally, we saw him at a concert in Oxford and decided it was time to say hello. His moon-face and humorous mouth broke into a large grin when we told him we thought he was haunting us. After that, we saw him often. Leo christened him 'Tosci, the Athletic Anarchist' because of his habit of conducting any music he was listening to (Tosci being short for Toscanini) and his keen participation in athletics, and his political leanings. 'The gutters shall run with their blood!' was his war-cry. Not, perhaps, to be taken totally seriously.

I had drifted willingly into going out with Leo. This very complex man, in his quiet way, had begun to exert considerable influence over me, and I didn't mind. He had joined the RAF in 1941, volunteering as a pilot. He reached ITW before a medical examination found that he had almost no sight in his left eye. That was the end of his aircrew ambitions of course. As he'd long been interested in radio, it seemed the natural thing to go into then. In spite of his vision he was an excellent shot and was interested in guns, too.

After a wireless operator's course, Leo applied for a wireless mechanic's course, spending time at Cranwell and Madley, Herefordshire, in the course of his training. Hoping to get away from Upper Heyford after the course, he was disappointed. Heyford liked to hold on to its well-qualified staff. And here he'd remained, despite other efforts to get away, including volunteering for overseas postings. After he described to me the conditions at Heyford earlier in the war, I wasn't surprised he'd tried for a posting; the discipline had been of pre-war standard. In comparison to an operational station it was harsh indeed, but it had eased a little by the time I arrived.

Periodically, Leo had to spend a week on duty at the

Bombing Range at Preston Capes, near Woodford Halse. While he was there, I finished a night duty, and having 36 hours off thought I would go and see him. I wasn't sure of the precise location – Woodford Halse was near Banbury I gathered, so I set out to hitch to Banbury, not feeling too tired. I reached Banbury without difficulty and a lorry driver set me down by the road which led to Woodford. I walked for what seemed like a very long way. A van came along, and stopped for me, but it was a grocery delivery van and only going a short way along the road. I was grateful for the short lift though. As I got down I asked the driver how far it was to Woodford. 'About two miles,' he told me. I walked on. It must have been two miles when I saw a farm-worker in a field and called to him: 'How far to Woodford Halse?' 'It'll be about two miles,' he said. I began to think I was in a sort of nightmare. Every time I asked how far it was, it would be two miles- maybe I should have gone to bed after all.

But I reached Woodford, and at last had some luck – the first person I saw was Leo! He was about to return to Preston Capes on the back of a colleague's motorcycle, but sent me ahead on the pillion instead. I was so thankful to be sitting down instead of on my feet, as we roared up the hill beneath the overhanging trees. Leo walked up, and collected me from the farmhouse where the bombing range staff were billeted. The farmer's wife had made me a welcome cup of tea. I was fascinated by the countryside around, which swept up into hills and down into hollows, making patterns of green crops and brown ploughed fields, the furrows making elegant curves on the upward-sweeping ground. Leo pointed out a commanding height with tall trees growing on the summit, telling me it was exactly the sort of place which prehistoric tribes would have used as a hill-fort. We went across to the range, situated on high ground, with a brick tower at either end where the bombs were plotted. Leo was on duty that evening and said I could come with him if I'd like to, and watch the bombing. I thought that would be interesting. He had another suggestion – that we asked the farmer's wife if she could put me up for the night! I hadn't booked out, but thought I may as well take a chance as I wasn't on duty till midday the next day.

She agreed, and took me to a room with a big brass bedstead and feather mattress, and a washstand with a basin and ewer of cold water. But first there was the bombing range. It was still light when we made our way there, down a lane and across fields until we reached the nearest tower. An R/T set stood on a table inside, and the duty airman answered as aircraft called-up. I stood outside, anxious to see what was going on. I was rather disappointed – there wasn't much to see. Some small yellow flashes as the practice bombs fell – little else. I could hear the aircraft, of course, and glimpse shapes against the darkening sky but it wasn't a busy evening. As we walked back across the fields to Grange Farm, we saw a barn owl flying silently across our path on white, ghostly wings.

It was a wonderful place for wildlife, Leo told me – only a day or so earlier, he had seen a family of kestrels on a fence – a most unusual sight. Other birds and animals abounded, and rabbits were everywhere. The men on the range often trapped them to eat – they did their own cooking in a small kitchen at the side of their quarters. Leo too had snared rabbits, until a day when he caught one in a wire snare he'd laid by a hedge. The snare held the rabbit's leg, and each time Leo tried to seize the animal it plunged through the hedge, the snare dragging at the leg until it was cut to the bone. He finally caught it and killed it quickly, but never laid another snare after that. There were mushrooms to be gathered in the early, dewy mornings at the right season, as well as blackberries. Sometimes there were eggs too, if the farmer's chickens escaped and decided to lay in the hedge and the RAF got there first!

I slept soundly and peacefully in my feather bed, and Leo woke me the next morning with a mug of tea. I had breakfast with the boys, and the one with the motorbike offered to run me back into Banbury. I hitched back to camp, and was relieved to find I hadn't been missed. I had enjoyed my brief stay in that remote and beautiful place. I needed such places. Perhaps the effects of four years in close confines with people – however congenial – were having their effect.

VE Day! The war in Europe was over at last. There was a

bonfire in the Parade Ground, and a dance in the NAAFI for all ranks. Leo and I went. He couldn't dance very well, but it didn't matter. He'd learn – and he did. We had a few drinks, but as only beer and cider was available in the NAAFI, I didn't drink much, and it was noticeable that the officers and sergeants who'd come soon disappeared to their respective Messes where they could imbibe stronger liquid! But it was a curiously muted celebration. It felt almost as if everyone was putting on an act. Perhaps we were. Perhaps too much had happened. So many people had died – so many known personally – and I couldn't forget the horror of the concentration camps.

Things went on much as before. We went on duty and came off – and the WAAF powers that be had a brainwave. All shift workers would now do a week of nights at a time, and a special hut would be set aside for us to sleep in so that we wouldn't be disturbed. Doing a week of nights together was supposed to be better for us – our bodies could adjust to the routine better or something. The fact that we'd been working the shifts we had for four years or whatever made it seem a little pointless, even more so when the tannoy in the hut blared out announcements and woke us up. 'Wouldn't be disturbed', indeed! 'Shall I stop it?' I enquired after the fourth time. The other disgruntled would-be sleepers chorused, 'Yes!' So I balanced a chair on a table under the speaker and inserted a pin between the terminals, remembering James' useful advice on the subject. That cured it, and we went back to sleep.

The year moved on to early summer. Classes in educational and vocational training were started: EVT. I thought I'd try maths classes as Jean's boy friend, Roy – another wireless operator – was taking them. He knew his subject and I tried – but equations remained a mystery to me. I never could grasp how it was that a letter X should suddenly equal a number. Apparently, everyone else could. I gave up. Maths had always defeated me. I was now so much happier at Heyford. Yet sometimes, for no reason that I could fathom, fits of depression caught up with me. At these times, if I had the leisure, I walked or cycled out into the countryside, finding solitude and natural surroundings the best and most complete restorative I knew.

There was an evening when, walking along a lane in the approaching dusk, I stopped by an old gate to look at a field of green corn. It swayed gently in the breath of wind that stirred and stilled. Colours of the landscape were vivid as they are only in the short space between sunset and dark. I was in an odd mood as, standing by the lusty hawthorn hedge, I stared up at a slender, young ash sapling next to the gate and down to the lush richness of grass, weed and flower mingling at the foot of the hedge. My gaze drifted again to the green, gentle sea of the corn. I was open and receptive to all the growth and vigour and beauty around me. I willed myself to be free of myself, wanting desperately to become a part of what I saw, to flow into it, to know – what? I couldn't tell, but felt it must be strange and magical as the evening light, still glowing clear and pure through the dusk.

It almost happened. Another moment, and I was sure I would have been free, but the silence was shattered by noisy footsteps along the road, and loud voices cut through the spell I had tried to lay around myself, and it was gone. I sighed. It would never have worked anyway – would it? I passed the two airmen and walked quickly back to camp. 'The spell was broken, the key denied me,' wrote Rupert Brooke in a poem about a similar experience. I knew exactly what he meant.

The atom bomb was dropped on Japan. The war was truly over – all over! There were more celebrations on camp, but again there was a feeling of flatness underneath the surface of slightly hysterical jollity. At least the killing was finished, terrible as the last stage had been with the atom bomb and the mushroom cloud. The thing that haunted my mind was the report of shadows fixed on a wall by radioactivity. How could something so insubstantial as a shadow become permanent? It was hard to understand, and the whole, too awful to contemplate. Our Mossies were still flying. There was still work to do, even if it now seemed towards no end. There was an evening when I came off duty at midnight feeling jaded and sticky with the heat. I met Elsa in 'Smokey Joe's' – the supper cookhouse in front of the hangars where we could get a meal after evening duty.

A full moon shone brilliantly in a clear, starry sky and the air was cool and soft. As Elsa and I walked down the road towards the WAAF Site, she said, 'Let's go for a walk!' I'd been thinking along the same lines. So we strolled down to the Middleton Stoney road, but turned off into the little wood at the corner, where we'd found wild strawberries earlier. It was black under the trees, but there were patches of moonlight where the trees thinned, and it was so quiet that we crept along not wanting to break the silence of the wood. The call of an owl made us start. The air was full of night scents, which drifted in layers like mist. We came out of the wood, crossed a field whitened by the moon and passed through a copse, then came to the road. We followed it back, revelling in the dewy feel of the air and the soft light pouring down over the landscape around us – it was perfect. Then, coming to the corner where we turned back to camp, among high grasses by the roadside we saw bright gleams of green light. Glow-worms! We were entranced. I had never seen them before, and was enchanted to observe that their green glow wasn't extinguished by the silver flood of moonlight. It was a magical night.

Going on duty the next afternoon, I found a distinctly prickly atmosphere in Control. There had been some news of release groups, and it hadn't been to any of the Control officers' liking. Earlier rumours had been of a speeding up of release, but now it seemed more like a slow down. Everyone was in a sort of limbo – still in the service, yet wanting to get started in civilian life since it was going to happen anyway. I wanted to get out too, but wasn't sure what I'd do. I'd have to sort something out. If only there had been a civilian airfield near home – I would have gone into airfield control because it was something I knew about and was interested in. But there wasn't an airfield anywhere in my area so I'd have to think again. I still didn't know when I'd be released. Perhaps several months yet. But eventually I heard. Every week now people were leaving. An edifice seemed to be crumbling. My turn was to come at the beginning of January 1946. On the appointed day I went to Wolverhampton to the Demob Centre, where I handed in all my kit except what I stood up in. We were allowed to keep that! I was given a money order for £12 to buy civilian clothes, and my gratuity of £42. I felt almost rich. Afterwards I took the train back to Oxford, but missed the bus to Buckingham. Well, there was somewhere I could go. I went to Upper Heyford the night I was demobbed. I knew Leo was on duty at the transmitting station, so I went there. Next day, I went home.

Leo finally achieved his ambition to leave Upper Heyford – he was posted to France, where he remained for the rest of the year. But on his first leave, we were married. Elsa went to Oxford – and got married. Sally and Joyce, now married, produced babies. Civilian life began again for us all.

It was a strange feeling.

Glossary

ACP	Airfield Control Pilot
ACW	Aircraftwoman (lowest WAAF rank)
AG	Air-gunner
BAT Flight	Blind Approach Training Flight
CC	Confined to barracks
CEMA	An organisation providing mainly classical music concerts to Service audiences
CO	Commanding Officer
Chance light	A powerful light at the end of the runway to assist landing and take-off. Made by Chance Bros
Darky	A call on R/T from an aircraft in trouble. Always answered by giving the name of the station receiving, i.e., 'This is Waddington'
DF	Direction Finding. W/T section in contact with aircraft in the air
DI	Daily Inspection
DROs	Daily Routine Orders
Erk	Slang for Aircraftman
EFTS	Elementary Flying School
ETA	Estimated Time of Arrival
FCO	Flying Control Officer
FFI	Free from Infection
FMU	Field Maintenance Unit
GC	Group Captain
Jankers	Extra duties by other ranks, often domestic
Kites	Aircraft
KRs	King's Regulations
LAC	Leading Aircraftman
LACW	Leading Aircraftwoman
MEF	Middle East Forces
MO	Medical Officer
MQ	Married Quarters
NAAFI	Navy, Army, Air Force Institute, where

	non-service meals and cigarettes could be obtained
NFT	Night Flying Test
Ops	Bombing operations. Also the Operations Section
OUT	Operational Training Unit
P/O	Pilot Officer
POW	Prisoner of War
RAAF	Royal Australian Air Force
RCAF	Royal Canadian Air Force
RFC	Royal Flying Corps
Rooinek	Rhodesian slang for Englishmen, meaning 'red-neck'
R/T	Radio Telephone
SFCO	Senior Flying Control Officer
SHQ	Station Headquarters
SP	Station Police
SRO	Station Routine Orders
'Tee Emm'	Training Manual for aircrew
u/t	Under Training
Utility	Small van
Wimpy	Wellington aircraft
Works and Bricks	Section responsible for the maintenance of airfield buildings
W/Op	Wireless operator
W/Op Ag	Wireless Operator/Air Gunner
W/T	Wireless Telegraphy
YW	Y.W.C.A. A hostel providing cheap accommodation

Witness to War books from Crécy Publishing

As the global conflicts of the 20th century move out of living memory, it becomes more and more difficult to understand the unique experiences of ordinary people trying to fight and survive in extraordinary circumstances. The everyday hardships, dangers, fears and heroism of these times cannot be conveyed any better than in the words of those who lived through these times, and best of all these stories are found in the Goodall 'Witness To War' series.

Enemy Coast Ahead
Guy Gibson

Leader of the Dambusters
First published in 1944, Guy Gibson's Enemy Coast Ahead quickly became regarded as the classic Bomber Command book, following Gibson's RAF career from flying the Hampden and Manchester at the beginning of WWII to the triumphant return home of the Lancasters from the famous 1943 Dambuster raid which Gibson led and for which he was awarded the Victoria Cross.

Enemy Coast Ahead is also the inside story of life in Bomber Command throughout the first years of WW2, culminating in breath-holding drama as the RAF planned, practiced and strove towards breaching the dams on that famous night in May 1943.

256 pages, 'B' format paperback
b&w photograph section
9 780907 579625 £6.99

'A remarkable piece of descriptive writing. It records the night-to-night life of a bomber pilot with modesty, humour and a rich understanding... everyone should read this unforgettable book.'
Punch

Evader
Denys Teare

On September 5th, 1943, Denys Teare baled out of his burning Lancaster bomber over Occupied France; and from this moment on became an evader in the midst of the enemy. Continually thwarted in his escape attempts, he was a doubly wanted man: not only a British airman evading the occupying force, but also an active member of the French Resistance.

This book tells what it was really like living in France under the Nazis, of the danger and horror before the Liberation – and of what liberation really meant when it came.

This new paperback edition includes material which originally came under censorship, and

is illustrated with photographs from the author's own collection.

240 pages, 'B' format paperback
b&w photograph section
9 780907 579485 £7.99

'Wonderful(ly) detailed story of life in occupied territory.'
GMR Talk – Manchester Local Radio

Flights into the Night
L Anthony Leicester

Tony Leicester was one of many high school graduates who trained as a pilot and at the tender age of nineteen found himself in charge of a crew setting out to make their contribution to winning the war. That training was minimal and accidents frequent becomes painfully evident as he takes us through his experiences in Canada, Europe and across the Middle East. Inexperience, unreliable aircraft and treacherous weather, to say nothing of a determined enemy, all conspired to severely test the skills, ingenuity and luck of these young aviators who, if they stayed alive, quickly became men..

224 pages, paperback
8 page b&w photograph section
9 780907 579687 £7.99

'A very easy to read, interesting book'. Air Gunners Association

'The monsoon, or chagara lasted three months. While it brought life-giving rains to farmers, to aircrew it was one long nightmare of horrendous thunderstorms, teeming rain and crackling lightning. Flying in this stuff it was every man for himself. Each of my crew had to find something strong to hang on to as we bounced and pitched through heavy turbulence, as if riding in a square-wheeled cart. Lightning flashes stabbed the clouds like flames from a Pittsburgh steel foundry. Each flash filled the Wellington's cockpit with dazzling blue light and froze all movement for a split second. But we had no choice but to fly on.'

Lancaster Target
Jack Currie

Described as one of the best three books about life in Bomber Command during World War Two, Lancaster Target is the classic story of one crew's fight to fl y and survive a full tour of operations in the night skies of wartime Europe. Flying Lancaster bombers from RAF Wickenby in Lincolnshire between 1943 and 1944, Jack Currie chronicles the life and death struggles against flak, night fighters and perilous weather with clarity and feeling, whilst capturing the 'live for the moment' spirit of off duty escapades.

192 pages, 'B' format paperback
8 page b&w photograph section
9 780907 579281 £7.99

'...rightly described as a classic.'
British Aerospace News

Mosquito Pathfinder
Albert and Ian Smith

Having suffered the devastating effects of the Manchester blitz, sixteen year old Salford lad Albert Smith signed up to join the RAF never thinking he would eventually survive 90 operations over hostile territory. His horizons immediately widened as he completed his training and began a first tour as a Wellington navigator over Germany and North Africa. Germany was full of flak whilst Africa was full of scorpions - all new and fearful experiences for a naïve young northerner. Following a brief respite at an operational training unit in Warboys, Smith volunteered for Pathfinder Mosquitoes with 109 Squadron at Little Staughton where, with the Oboe navigation system in its infancy, he was soon in action illuminating bombing targets.

Over 52 Pathfinder operations, we relive successes and failures with the new target marking system; triumphs and disappointments, mission aborts and successes, and all the fears and nervousness entailed in being the first aircraft over a heavily defended target. His poignant narrative interspersed with extracts from official Bomber Command records combine to give both the official and human story of the air war over Germany and beyond.

240 pages, 'B' format paperback
4 page b&w photograph section
9 780907 579786 £7.99

Nine Lives
Al Deere

The renowned autobiography of New Zealand's most famous RAF pilot who saw action from the Munich Crisis to the invasion of France in 1944. Al Deere experienced the drama of the early days of the Battle of Britain while serving with Spitfire squadrons based at Hornchurch and Manston, and his compelling story tells of the successes and frustrations of those critical weeks.

Deere was in action over Dunkirk for 14 days in May 1940 during which time he shot down six enemy aircraft including a Me 109 and his nine lives are the accounts of his fantastic luck in escaping from seemingly impossible situations.

288 pages, 'B' format paperback
8 page b&w photograph section
9 780907 579823 £7.99

'...undoubtedly one of the classics of the genre, giving an excellent firsthand account of Dunkirk and the Battle of Britain.'
Pilot Magazine

No Moon Tonight
Don Charlwood

Accepted as a RAF navigator in 1940, Don Charlwood was posted to 103 Squadron at Elsham Wolds in the winter of 1942. There he crewed up with a pilot from Western Australia and a British crew to fly a Lancaster bomber. In No Moon Tonight he gives a profound insight into the inner lives of the men of Bomber Command and their hopes and fears in the face of mounting losses. He depicts the appalling human cost of the air war in an account which has been favourably compared to enduring memoirs of the 1st World War, namely Sassoon's Memoirs of an Infantry Officer and Remarque's All Quiet on the Western Front. A memorable first hand account of the air war over Germany.

224 pages, 'B' format paperback
8 page b&w photograph section
9 780907 579977 £7.99

'...the tension is so sustained and vivid that the book hangs together, emotionally like a piece of music.'
Daily Telegraph

Pathfinder
Air Vice-Marshal Don Bennett

Vice-Marshal Donald Bennett CB, CBE, DSO, – was one of the most outstanding figures in RAF Bomber Command in World War II and the creator and leader of the legendary Pathfinder Force of No. 8 Group. His record as a brilliant pilot and one of the world's greatest air navigators made him the obvious choice as leader of the Pathfinders –

the élite force designed to carry out pioneering target-marking and precision-bombing of Nazi occupied Europe.

From the date of its inception almost every RAF Main Force attack was led by the Pathfinders. Night after night they spearheaded Bomber Command's assault on major German targets using increasingly sophisticated devices, including radar, to improve the efficiency of the bombing operations. Bennett also played a prominent part in deploying a Mosquito intruder force to harass Germany by night and also in developing FIDO, the invaluable fog dispersal system. By the end of the war he was commanding a total of 19 squadrons of the Pathfinder Force.

In July 1942 Group Captain Don Bennett was appointed Pathfinder Leader by Bomber Command. Two years later, at the age of 33, he became the youngest Air Vice-Marshal in the history of the RAF. He was appointed CBE in 1943 and CB in 1944. He died in 1986.

272 pages, paperback
8 page b&w photograph section
9 780907 579571 £7.99

'...one of the most brilliant airmen of his generation: an outstanding pilot, a superb navigator who was also capable of stripping a wireless set or overhauling an engine.'
Wikipedia

Rear Gunner Pathfinders
Ron Smith DFM
Foreword by Group Captain Hamish Mahaddie DSO DFC AFC & BAR

A Bomber Command book with a difference, the story of the air war over Germany as seen from the small Perspex bubble of a 'Tail-End Charlie' rear gunner in a Lancaster. Flying firstly with 626 squadron, and later 156 Pathfinder squadron, Ron Smith flew 65 operations and recorded them with the intensity brought on by the isolation of being cocooned in his lonely gun turret.

160 pages, 'B' format paperback
b&w photograph section
9 780907 579274 £7.99

'Suddenly we were over the Big City... after long hours of searching the night sky from the coast, to be suddenly propelled into the brilliant hell over Berlin produced a freezing of the mind...flak sliced up through the broken illuminated clouds, ascending gracefully to stream past the turret. A Lancaster slid across at right angles with a single fighter just behind it, as if attached by an invisible

thread... the city far below was bubbling and boiling, splashes of fire opening out as the blockbusters pierced this terrible brew.'

Wing Leader
Air Vice-Marshal 'Johnnie' Johnson

The thrilling story of the top-scoring Allied fighter pilot of WWII. 'Johnnie' Johnson served with Fighter Command squadrons throughout the war, scoring his 38th and final victory in September 1944. From the moment the author joins his first operational Spitfire squadron in August 1940, the reader is taken on an epic journey through the great aerial battles of the war, from the Battle of Britain to the bitter fighting over Dieppe, and into the final offensive over the skies of occupied France. Finally crossing the Rhine into Germany as a group captain, 'Johnnie' Johnson commanded a wing of the latest and most powerful Spitfires. This is his story in his own words.

320 pages, paperback
16 page b&w photograph section
9 780907 579878 £7.99

'It is the stuff that heroes are made of'
Aviation News
'Wing Leader is a must read for anyone interested in 'Johnnie' Johnson, or the daily workings of the RAF in WWII.'
www.dogfighter.com

Wings Over Georgia
Jack Currie

Jack Currie tells the story of his entry into the RAF during WWII, his early UK training and his initial training with the US Army Air Corps under the Arnold Scheme which led to his first solo and the eventual achievement of that coveted pair of wings. Training complete, Jack returned to England to meet the men who were to be his Lancaster crew and relates their experiences in *Lancaster Target* above. Written in his inimitable style, *Wings over Georgia* is packed with incident as he writes perceptively about the serious side of flying interspersed with hilarious accounts of his off-duty moments.

156 pages, 178mm x 111mm
b&w photograph section
9 780907 5791113 £3.99

Order online at www.crecy.co.uk or telephone +44 (0) 161 499 0024
Crécy Publishing 1a Ringway Trading Est, Shadowmoss Rd, Manchester, M22 5LH
enquiries@crecy.co.uk